# EVERYDAY'S A
# SUNDAE

ISBN 978-0-933477-50-6

All rights reserved. Printed in Canada.

EDITOR: Adrienne Gagnier
DESIGN: Tony Morello | morellowebdesign.com

www.thechefsconnection.com

Distributed in the United States by Chefs Connection, New York, NY; Published by Alan "Battman", Batt.
Recipes/ Texts ©2017 by Stephen Collucci. Photographs ©2017 by Battman.

FALL

WINTER

# FOREWORD
## by Michael Laiskonis

### I scream, you scream...

I must confess that I am a bit of a nerd when it comes to ice cream. My history with ice cream is probably like that of most other cooks: from not really knowing what I was doing to becoming fully obsessed with its inner workings. As one begins to grasp a better understanding of ice cream, it becomes at once easier and oddly far more difficult. The more you know, the more you realize you don't know. Yet, armed with a few basics and the right equipment, the options are endless. From low-brow guilty pleasures to high-brow inventiveness, ice cream is my favorite vehicle for carrying flavor and texture.

Most restaurant pastry chefs include a frozen element in nearly every composed dessert on their menus, and though it may be more than just an obligatory afterthought, rarely is it the focal point of the dish. In this playful book, Stephen makes ice cream the star. Included are numerous recipes and preparations cast as supporting actors to further elevate his ideas, creating a whole greater than the sum of its parts. These base recipes may be simple on the surface, but represent the obsessive spirit of the professional pastry chef – where most books would be fine with suggesting store-bought graham crackers, Stephen encourages his readers to make their own.

With a rock-solid pastry pedigree working in some of New York City's best kitchens, Stephen's style has evolved into one that never really goes out of 'style'. He has a knack for honoring modern classics – putting his own personal stamp on an idea, yet never overthinking it to the point of unfamiliarity. A lot of cooking is simply sourcing the best possible raw ingredients and thoughtfully coaxing out what they want to express. That's not as easy as it sounds. And with all the technical wizardry pastry chefs often apply to their creations, that essence of the raw material is easily lost. Stephen manages to balance these two tendencies in a way that eludes many others. The true skill of a good technician is in some ways the art of deception – making the results look effortless, no matter how much tinkering takes place behind the scenes.

I often like to think of pastry chefs as peddlers of nostalgia. We all harbor deep, hard-wired associations with sweetness, and as masters of the medium, pastry chefs have the unique power to tap into that nostalgia. Ice cream is the perfect portal into one's childhood memories, whether we're conscious of it or not. Stephen's approach to ice cream is both highly refined, yet approachable; rather than serve forth flavors that may challenge us, these are dishes you want to eat. In a profession where European traditions largely dictate our sensibilities and an ever-expanding pantry of global flavors compete for our palate's attention, I see Stephen's take on contemporary dessert as his own personal expression of 'Americana'. And the great thing about celebrating our own homegrown traditions is that we all experience these traditions in diverse ways. I like the idea that ice cream is perhaps the most democratic of desserts. Indeed, we all scream for it!

**Michael Laiskonis**
**Creative Director**
Institute of Culinary Education

# STEPHEN COLLUCCI

### I grew up in a brick house at 66 Elm Road in Newark.

My dad's parents lived at number 64½, not just on the same street, and not just on the same block, but literally next door. While my parents went to church on Sundays, as a kid of three I would stay back and help my grandparents prepare Sunday dinner, not an unfamiliar thing to do for most Italian families across the great state of New Jersey.

Cousins, aunts, and uncles would turn up on those Sunday afternoons to "mangia" on braciola, lasagna, and the likes. It was every bit the stereotypical Italian-American upbringing, and I wouldn't have had it any other way.

Perhaps it's no surprise that the kid who sat peeling garlic and rolling meatballs at his grandmother's kitchen table before he went to kindergarten grew up to revere food. Living next door to grandma and grandpa had some amazing perks such as sunny-side up eggs for breakfast daily, and countless Friday night sleepovers. Being Pop's sidekicks greeted us with endless treats like potato and eggs, pepperoni pizza, and you guessed it-ice cream.

Most days out on his coattails ended with a trip to Nasto's ice cream parlor, where more often than not he would ask for a pint of everything they had to offer and we would gorge ourselves on everything from cherry-vanilla to pistachio. It's no wonder I love ice cream; it must be genetic.

Need more proof? I have never seen my father concentrate as much as he does when he's concocting one of his everything-but the-kitchen sink sundaes. Some of my fondest childhood memories are made of spending time with my grandparents and eating lemon ice-the real stuff.

Enjoy these recipes while you create delicious memories of your own, sprinkled with laughter, and a cherry on top.

### Stephen Collucci

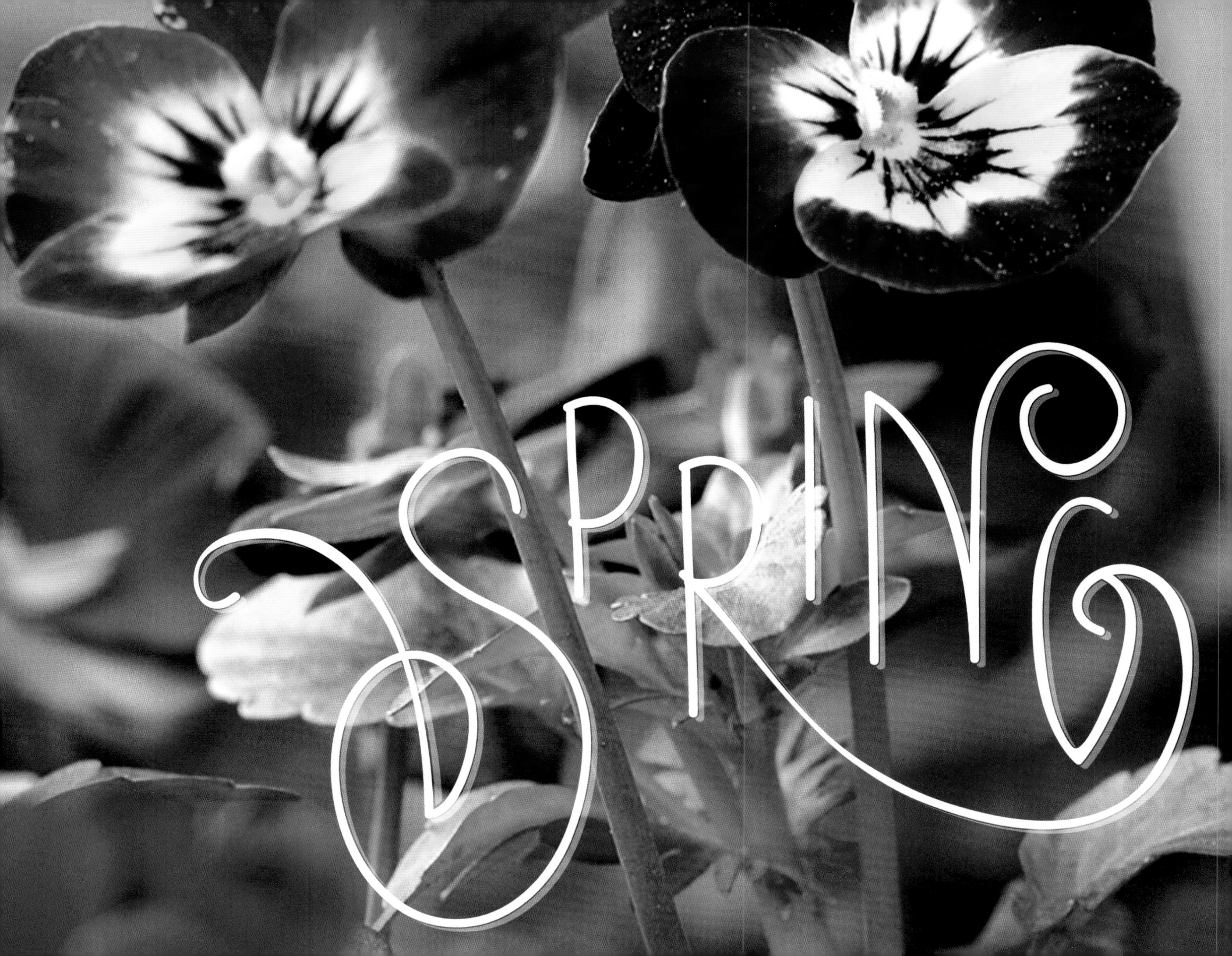
SPRING

# CANNOLI ICE CREAM

## CANNOLI ICE CREAM

9 LARGE EGG YOLKS
1 QUART MILK
2 CUPS RICOTTA
1½ CUPS SUGAR
1 PINCH OF CINNAMON
½ TEASPOON VANILLA
¼ TEASPOON ORANGE ZEST
¾ TEASPOON SALT
½ CUP CRUSHED CANNOLI SHELL
½ CUP MINI CHOCOLATE CHIPS

1. In a medium heavy-bottomed pot, combine the milk, cream, half of the sugar, and fresh ginger.
2. Bring the mixture to a full rolling boil.
3. Meanwhile, whisk together the remaining sugar and the egg yolks until the sugar is dissolved, about 30 seconds to one minute.
4. After the milk mixture has reached a rolling boil, carefully stream the liquid into the egg yolks, whisking constantly to prevent curdling. Add the salt.
5. Chill the ice cream base on an ice bath. Refrigerate the ice cream base overnight allowing the fresh ginger to steep.
6. Strain the base through a fine-mesh sieve into a clean container, discarding fresh ginger.
7. Freeze in an ice cream machine according to manufacturer instructions, then fold the chopped
8. candied ginger into the ice cream before placing in the freezer.

## CANNOLI DOUGH

1 CUP ALL PURPOSE FLOUR
1 TABLESPOON SOFT UNSALTED BUTTER
1 PINCH OF SALT
½ TEASPOON SUGAR
¼ TEASPOON WHITE WINE

1. In a kitchenaid mixer fitted with a paddle attachment, combine all ingredients until smooth.
2. Let dough rest, covered, at room temperature for 15-20 minutes.
3. On a lightly floured surface, roll the cannoli dough to about ¼-inch thick and chill.
4. Cut the dough into ½-inch strips and fry in 350 degree oil until golden brown.
5. Blot excess oil off with paper towels if needed.

# ALMOND MILK SORBET with Biscotti

## ALMOND MILK SORBET

1 CUP WHOLE ALMONDS, TOASTED
4 CUPS WATER
1 VANILLA BEAN, SCRAPED
1 TEASPOON SALT
1 CUP SIMPLE SYRUP
½ CUP MAPLE SYRUP
1 PINCH OF CINNAMON, OPTIONAL

1. Using a high speed blender, blend the almonds and water for several minutes until the milk is smooth and creamy.
2. Strain the almond milk through cheese cloth, or a nut milk bag.
3. Add the remaining ingredients to the strained almond milk.
4. Freeze in an ice cream machine according to manufacturer instructions.

## BISCOTTI

2 CUP ALL PURPOSE FLOUR
1 CUP SUGAR
1 TEASPOON BAKING POWDER
2 EGG
1 PINCH OF SALT
1 TEASPOON GROUND STAR ANISE

1. In a kitchenaid mixer fitted with a paddle attachment, combine the sugar and egg. Mix until smooth.
2. Add the remaining ingredients. Mix until combined scraping down the sides of the bowl.
3. Divide the dough into two pieces and form each piece into a log the length of your sheet pan by rolling on a floured surface. Place the logs onto a parchment-lined sheet pan and press the dough down slightly until it is about a ½-inch in thickness.
4. Bake for about 15-20 minutes until the biscotti is golden brown.
5. When the biscotti is cool enough to handle, cut the logs into ½-inch slices.
6. Place the biscotti slices, cut-side up, onto the baking sheet and bake for an additional 5-10 minutes, until lightly toasted.

# COFFEE NIB CRUNCH SUNDAE with Amaretti Cookies and Kahlua Hot Fudge

### COFFEE NIB ICE CREAM

9 LARGE EGG YOLKS
2 CUPS WHOLE MILK
2 CUPS HEAVY CREAM
1 CUP COFFEE BEANS

¾ CUP PLUS 2 TABLESPOONS SUGAR
¾ TEASPOON SALT
¾ CUP CRUSHED COCOA NIB BRITTLE

1. In a medium heavy-bottomed pot, combine the milk, cream, coffee beans, and half of the sugar. Bring the mixture to a full rolling boil.
2. Meanwhile, whisk together the remaining sugar and the egg yolks until the sugar is dissolved, about 30 seconds to one minute.
3. After the milk mixture has reached a rolling boil, carefully stream the liquid into the egg yolks, whisking constantly to prevent curdling. Add the salt.
4. Chill the ice cream base on an ice bath. Refrigerate the ice cream base overnight, allowing the coffee beans to steep.
5. Strain the base through a fine-mesh sieve into a clean container.
6. Freeze in an ice cream machine according to manufacturer instructions then fold the crushed cocoa nib brittle into the ice cream before placing in the freezer.

### COCOA NIB BRITTLE

1 CUP SUGAR
2 TABLESPOONS WATER
2 TABLESPOONS LIGHT CORN SYRUP
½ STICK UNSALTED BUTTER

2 TEASPOONS SALT
¼ TEASPOON BAKING SODA
⅓ CUP COCOA NIBS

1. In a medium heavy-bottomed pot, combine the sugar, water, corn syrup, and butter. Meanwhile, set aside two silpats or pieces of parchment, and a rolling pin on a heat-resistant surface.
2. Begin to cook the mixture over medium heat, watching carefully until it becomes a light amber color. Be sure to not stir or agitate the mixture once it begins to boil to avoid crystallizing.
3. Once the caramel has reached the desired color, lower the heat and add the baking soda and salt (the mix will foam up slightly). Mix until combined and continue to cook until the caramel is a medium amber color, about 30 seconds to one minute.
4. Remove the pot from the heat and carefully stir in the cocoa nibs. Pour immediately onto the prepared silpat or parchment, topping with the second silpat or piece of parchment paper.
5. Use the rolling pin, roll out the sandwiched brittle until it is about ¼-inch in thickness and uniform. Let cool, and break into pieces, as you desire. Store in an airtight container for 1-2 weeks.

### AMARETTI COOKIE

2½ CUPS ALL PURPOSE FLOUR
1 PINCH OF SALT
2 STICKS UNSALTED BUTTER
½ CUP ALMOND PASTE
1 TEASPOON BAKING POWDER

1 CUP SUGAR
1 EGG
3 TABLESPOONS AMARETTO
CINNAMON SUGAR

1. In a kitchenaid mixer fitted with a paddle attachment, combine the sugar, butter, and almond paste and cream until smooth.
2. Add the egg and amaretto. Mix until combined scraping down the sides of the bowl.
3. Add the salt and flour. Mix until combined scraping down the sides of the bowl once or twice to ensure the dough is homogeneous.
4. Refrigerate until the dough is chilled.
5. Once the dough is chilled, scoop tablespoon-sized portions and roll into rounds.
6. Toss the dough rounds in the cinnamon sugar until evenly coated and place on a greased or parchment lined baking sheetpan. Bake at 350 degrees until the cookies are golden brown, about 8-10 minutes, rotating the sheetpan halfway through the baking process.
7. Let cool.

### CINNAMON SUGAR

2 CUPS SUGAR

1 TEASPOON GROUND CINNAMON

1. Combine ingredients in a bowl and mix until combined.

### KAHLUA FUDGE SAUCE

½ CUP WATER
¼ CUP SUGAR
1 STICK UNSALTED BUTTER
1 PINCH OF SALT
1 TEASPOON VANILLA

2 TABLESPOONS MAPLE SYRUP
¼ CUP KAHLUA (OR MORE IF YOU'RE FEELING FRISKY!)
⅓ CUP COCOA POWDER
¼ CUP BITTERSWEET CHOCOLATE

1. In a medium heavy-bottomed pot over medium-low heat, combine the butter and water. Melt.
2. Add the chocolate, sugar, maple syrup, and cocoa powder. Continue to cook until melted, and bring to a boil. Be careful to not scorch the bottom of the pot.
3. Remove the pot from the heat. Add the salt, vanilla, and Kahlua. Once cool, strain through a fine-mesh sieve. Keep refrigerated for 1-2 weeks.
4. In a bowl or a sundae glass, layer scoops of coffee nib ice cream with crushed amaretti cookieand top with Kahlua fudge.

# GINGER ICE CREAM with Rhubarb Chutney

## GINGER ICE CREAM

1 CUP FRESH GINGER ROOT, PEELED AND CHOPPED INTO SMALL PIECES
9 LARGE EGG YOLKS
2 CUPS WHOLE MILK
2 CUPS HEAVY CREAM
¾ CUP PLUS 2 TABLESPOONS SUGAR
¾ TEASPOON SALT
½ CUP CANDIED GINGER, FINELY CHOPPED

1. In a medium heavy-bottomed pot, combine the milk, cream, half of the sugar, and fresh ginger. Bring the mixture to a full rolling boil.
2. Meanwhile, whisk together the remaining sugar and the egg yolks until the sugar is dissolved, about 30 seconds to one minute.
3. After the milk mixture has reached a rolling boil, carefully stream the liquid into the egg yolks, whisking constantly to prevent curdling. Add the salt.
4. Chill the ice cream base on an ice bath. Refrigerate the ice cream base overnight allowing the fresh ginger to steep.
5. Strain the base through a fine-mesh sieve into a clean container, discarding fresh ginger.
6. Freeze in an ice cream machine according to manufacturer instructions, then fold the chopped candied ginger into the ice cream before placing in the freezer.

## RHUBARB CHUTNEY

4 CUPS CHOPPED RHUBARB (ABOUT 1½ POUNDS FRESH RHUBARB)
1½ CUPS SUGAR
½ CUP WATER
HALF OF A LEMON, ZESTED

1. Toss all ingredients in a large bowl and set aside for one hour.
2. Place the rhubarb mix in a medium heavy-bottomed pot, and bring to a boil over medium-high heat.
3. Stir rhubarb consistently for about 5 minutes, to make sure it won't scorch on the bottom of the pot.
4. Lower heat to medium-low, keeping your chutney at a constant simmer and stirring frequently, about 15-20 minutes; the rhubarb should be very soft, and the chutney should be thickened.
5. Chill chutney over an ice bath until cool. It can be used immediately, or refrigerated for several days.

# LEMON-BASIL SORBET

1 CUP LEMON JUICE
2 CUPS SIMPLE SYRUP
½ CUP WATER
15-20 LARGE BASIL LEAVES
1 PINCH OF SALT

1.  In a medium heavy bottomed pot bring the simple syrup to a boil and add the basil leaves.
    Turn off the heat and steep for 15-20 minutes. Strain.
2.  Combine the remaining ingredients.
3.  Freeze in an ice cream machine according to manufacturer instructions.

# MINT COOKIE ICE CREAM

## MINT COOKIE ICE CREAM

9 LARGE EGG YOLKS
2 CUPS WHOLE MILK
2 CUPS HEAVY CREAM
¾ CUP PLUS 2 TABLESPOONS SUGAR
¾ TEASPOON SALT
1 BUNCH FRESH MINT
1 CUP MINT COOKIE, CHOPPED
GREEN FOOD COLORING IF / AS DESIRED

1. In a medium heavy-bottomed pot, combine the whole milk, heavy cream, fresh mint, and half of the sugar. Bring the mixture to a full rolling boil.
2. Meanwhile, whisk together the remaining sugar and the egg yolks until the sugar is dissolved, about 30 seconds to one minute.
3. After the milk mixture has reached a rolling boil, carefully stream the liquid into the egg yolks, whisking constantly to prevent curdling. Add the salt and food coloring, if using.
4. Chill the ice cream base on an ice bath. Refrigerate the ice cream base overnight.
5. Strain the base through a fine-mesh sieve into a clean container.
6. Freeze in an ice cream machine according to manufacturer instructions, then fold the chopped mint cookie into the ice cream before placing in the freezer.

## CHOCOLATE SABLÉ

2 STICKS UNSALTED BUTTER
1 EGG
½ CUP SUGAR
1¼ CUP ALL PURPOSE FLOUR
⅓ CUP PLUS 1 TABLESPOON COCOA POWDER
1 PINCH OF SALT

1. In a kitchenaid mixer fitted with a paddle attachment, combine the sugar and butter, cream until smooth.
2. Add the egg. Mix until combined, scraping down the sides of the bowl.
3. Add the remaining ingredients and mix just until combined.

4. Sandwich the dough in between two pieces of parchment paper and using a rolling pin, roll the dough to about ¼-inch in thickness. Chill.
5. Once the dough is chilled, remove the top sheet of parchment and bake at 350 degrees until the dough is baked though, approximately 10 minutes, rotating halfway between baking.
6. Let cool.

## MINT BUTTERCREAM

½ CUP SHORTENING
1 CUP BUTTER
1 CUP CONFECTIONER'S SUGAR
1½ TEASPOONS PEPPERMINT EXTRACT
1 PINCH OF SALT

1. In a kitchenaid mixer fitted with a paddle attachment, combine all ingredients, and cream until smooth.
2. Store in an airtight container for 1-2 weeks.

## TO ASSEMBLE MINT COOKIE:

1. Cut the sheet of cooled chocolate sablé approximately in half.
2. Using an offset spatula, spread a generous amount of mint buttercream onto one half of the chocolate sablé, approximately ¼-inch in thickness.
3. Make a sandwich by topping the buttercream with the remaining half of chocolate sablé. Chill.
4. Once the layered cookie has chilled, chop into pieces of desired size and keep cold until needed for ice cream.

# PISTACHIO ICE CREAM CRÊPES

## PISTACHIO ICE CREAM

9 LARGE EGG YOLKS
2 CUPS WHOLE MILK
2 CUPS HEAVY CREAM
¾ CUP PLUS 2 TABLESPOONS SUGAR
¾ TEASPOON SALT
¼ CUP PLUS 2 TABLESPOONS PISTACHIO PASTE
½ CUP PISTACHIOS TOASTED, AND COARSELY CHOPPED

1. In a medium heavy-bottomed pot, combine the whole milk, heavy cream, pistachio paste, and half of the sugar. Bring the mixture to a full rolling boil.
2. Meanwhile, whisk together the remaining sugar and the egg yolks until the sugar is dissolved, about 30 seconds to one minute.
3. After the milk mixture has reached a rolling boil, carefully stream the liquid into the egg yolks, whisking constantly to prevent curdling. Add the salt.
4. Chill the ice cream base on an ice bath. Refrigerate the ice cream base overnight.
5. Strain the base through a fine-mesh sieve into a clean container.
6. Freeze in an ice cream machine according to manufacturer instructions, then fold the chopped pistachios into the ice cream before placing in the freezer.

## CRÊPES

6 EGGS
2 CUPS WHOLE MILK
1½ CUPS ALL PURPOSE FLOUR
½ TEASPOON VANILLA EXTRACT
1 PINCH OF SALT

1. In a kitchenaid mixer fitted with a whip attachment, begin to mix the flour and eggs on low speed.
2. Gradually add the milk, vanilla, and salt. Beat until smooth and lump-free.
3. Heat a lightly greased frying pan or griddle over medium heat.
4. Pour approximately a ¼-cup of crêpe batter onto the pan and tilt with circular motions to coat evenly.
5. Cook each crêpe for 1-2 minutes, or until the bottom is a golden brown. Loosen with a spatula and flip to cook the remaining side.
6. Fold crêpes as desired and fill with generous scoops of pistachio ice cream.
7. Dust with confectioner's sugar.

## STRAWBERRY HIBISCUS SORBET

3 CUPS PURÉED STRAWBERRIES (APPROXIMATELY 5 CUPS WHOLE STRAWBERRIES)
1½ CUPS SIMPLE SYRUP
1 PINCH OF SALT
1 TABLESPOON LEMON JUICE
3 TABLESPOONS HIBISCUS LEAVES

1. In a small heavy-bottomed pot, bring the simple syrup to a boil.
2. Add the hibiscus leaves and let steep for 20 minutes. Strain.
3. Add the remaining ingredients.
4. Freeze in an ice cream machine according to manufacturer instructions.

# STRAWBERRY HIBISCUS SORBET

3 CUPS PURÉED STRAWBERRIES (APPROXIMATELY 5 CUPS WHOLE STRAWBERRIES)
1½ CUPS SIMPLE SYRUP
1 PINCH OF SALT
1 TABLESPOON LEMON JUICE
3 TABLESPOONS HIBISCUS LEAVES

1.  In a small heavy-bottomed pot, bring the simple syrup to a boil.
2.  Add the hibiscus leaves and let steep for 20 minutes. Strain.
3.  Add the remaining ingredients.
4.  Freeze in an ice cream machine according to manufacturer instructions.

# PEANUT BUTTER COOKIE ICE CREAM

## PEANUT BUTTER COOKIE ICE CREAM

1 QUART WHOLE MILK
½ CUP DARK BROWN SUGAR
¼ CUP PLUS 2 TABLESPOONS SUGAR
¾ TEASPOON SALT
1 CUP SMOOTH PEANUT BUTTER
1 TEASPOON VANILLA EXTRACT
1 CUP PEANUT BUTTER COOKIE DOUGH, CHILLED AND ROUGHLY CHOPPED

1. In a medium heavy-bottomed pot, combine the milk, brown sugar, and peanut butter. Bring the mixture to a full rolling boil.
2. Meanwhile, whisk together the sugar and the egg yolks until the sugar is dissolved, about 30 seconds to one minute.
3. After the milk mixture has reached a rolling boil, carefully stream the liquid into the egg yolks, whisking constantly to prevent curdling. Add the salt and vanilla extract.
4. Chill the ice cream base on an ice bath. Refrigerate the ice cream base overnight.
5. Strain the base through a fine-mesh sieve into a clean container.
6. Freeze in an ice cream machine according to manufacturer instructions then fold the chopped peanut butter cookie dough into the ice cream before placing in the freezer.

## PEANUT BUTTER COOKIE DOUGH

1 CUP ALL PURPOSE FLOUR
1 PINCH OF SALT
¼ CUP PEANUT BUTTER
¾ STICK UNSALTED BUTTER
½ TEASPOON VANILLA EXTRACT
¼ CUP SUGAR
¼ CUP DARK BROWN SUGAR

1. In a kitchenaid mixer fitted with a paddle attachment, combine the sugars, butter, and peanut butter and cream until smooth.
2. Add the salt, vanilla, and flour and mix until combined, scraping down the sides of the bowl once or twice to ensure the dough is homogeneous.
3. Sandwich the dough between two pieces of parchment paper, and using a rolling pin, roll the dough to about ¼-inch in thickness. Chill.
4. Once the dough is chilled, chop into pieces as desired to fold into the ice cream.
5. Refrigerate until needed.

# ROCKY ROAD BANANA SPLIT

ONE RIPE BANANA (OR IF YOU LOVE UNDER-RIPE BANANAS, WE WON'T JUDGE!)
SCOOPS OF ROCKY ROAD ICE CREAM
MILK CHOCOLATE SAUCE
WHIPPED CREAM

1. In a wide bowl, layer scoops of rocky road ice cream on top of the banana.
2. Drizzle with milk chocolate sauce and top with whipped cream. Enjoy!

## ROCKY ROAD ICE CREAM

9 LARGE EGG YOLKS
2 CUPS WHOLE MILK
2 CUPS HEAVY CREAM
¾ CUP PLUS 2 TABLESPOONS SUGAR
¾ TEASPOON SALT

½ CUP CHOPPED DARK CHOCOLATE
½ CUP CHOPPED MILK CHOCOLATE
½ CUP TOASTED ALMONDS, FINELY CHOPPED
¾ CUP MARSHMALLOW SWIRL

1. Place the milk and dark chocolate in a large bowl and set aside.
2. In a medium heavy-bottomed pot, combine the milk, cream, and half of the sugar. Bring the mixture to a full rolling boil.
3. Meanwhile, whisk together the remaining sugar and the egg yolks until the sugar is dissolved, about 30 seconds to one minute.
4. After the milk mixture has reached a rolling boil, carefully pour half of the hot milk over chocolate, and whisk until chocolate is completely combined.
5. Add the remaining hot milk and whisk together. Add salt.
6. Strain the base through a fine-mesh sieve into a clean container.
7. Chill the ice cream base on an ice bath. Refrigerate the ice cream base overnight.
8. Freeze in an ice cream machine according to manufacturer instructions, then fold in chopped almonds and marshmallow swirl before placing in the freezer.

## MARSHMALLOW SWIRL

1¾ CUPS SUGAR
2 TABLESPOONS LIGHT CORN SYRUP
½ CUP WATER

½ TEASPOON POWDERED GELATIN
4 LARGE EGG WHITES, ROOM TEMPERATURE

1. In a small pot, combine sugar, corn syrup, and ¼-cup water. Bring to a boil over high heat.
2. Boil until sugar mixture registers 240 degrees on a candy thermometer, to 'softball sugar' stage. Avoid stirring the sugar, in order to prevent crystallizing.
3. Meanwhile, put the other ¼-cup of water into a small bowl, and sprinkle with gelatin. Let gelatin soften and begin to dissolve, about 5 minutes.
4. Add the softened gelatin and water to the cooked sugar syrup once it has reached 240 degrees. Whisk to combine.
5. Put egg whites in a kitchenaid bowl fitted with a whisk attachment, and beat on high until frothy.
6. With mixer on low speed, slowly stream the hot sugar syrup into the egg whites. Gradually increase to high speed, and beat until marshmallow swirl is bright white and fluffy, about 5 minutes.
7. Let marshmallow swirl cool before using, about 30 minutes, or store in an airtight container up to one day.

*Alternatively, marshmallow swirl can be made using one half-sheet of silver sheet gelatin. Combine all of water with sugars in the pot to start, and bring to a boil. Meanwhile, soften gelatin in cold water, and whisk into sugar syrup once sugar reaches 240 degrees. Proceed with remainder of recipe.*

## TOASTED ALMONDS

1 CUP WHOLE ALMONDS

1. Preheat oven to 350 degrees.
2. Place almonds on a baking sheet, and toast until golden, about 7-10 minutes.
3. Cool and store in an airtight container until ready to use.

## MILK CHOCOLATE SAUCE

1 CUP DARK CHOCOLATE
1 CUP MILK CHOCOLATE
ONE PINCH SALT
1 TEASPOON VANILLA

1¾ CUP CREAM
¾ CUP MILK
½ CUP MAPLE SYRUP

1. In a medium heavy-bottomed pot over medium-low heat, combine the vanilla, cream, milk and maple syrup.
2. Add the chocolate and salt. Continue to cook until melted, and bring to a boil. Be careful to not scorch the bottom of the pot.
3. Remove the pot from the heat. Once cool, strain through a fine-mesh sieve. Keep refrigerated for up to one week.

## WHIPPED CREAM

1 CUP HEAVY CREAM

2 TEASPOONS CONFECTIONER'S SUGAR

1. In a kitchenaid mixer fitted with a whip attachment, combine the cream and sugar.
2. Beat at medium speed until medium-stiff peaks form.
3. Use immediately, or refrigerate for several hours until needed.

# CHAMOMILE ICE CREAM

9 LARGE EGG YOLKS
2 CUPS WHOLE MILK
2 CUPS HEAVY CREAM
1 BUNCH FRESH CHAMOMILE FLOWERS
¾ CUP PLUS 2 TABLESPOONS SUGAR
¾ TEASPOON SALT

1. In a medium heavy-bottomed pot, combine the milk, cream, chamomile flowers, and half of the sugar. Bring the mixture to a full rolling boil.
2. Meanwhile, whisk together the remaining sugar and the egg yolks until the sugar is dissolved, about 30 seconds to one minute.
3. After the milk mixture has reached a rolling boil, carefully stream the liquid into the egg yolks, whisking constantly to prevent curdling. Add the salt.
4. Chill the ice cream base on an ice bath. Refrigerate the ice cream base overnight allowing the chamomile to steep.
5. Strain the base through a fine-mesh sieve into a clean container, and discard the chamomile.
6. Freeze in an ice cream machine according to manufacturer instructions.

SUMMER

# APRICOT-BRANDY SORBET with Angel Food Cake

## APRICOT-BRANDY SORBET

2 POUNDS VERY RIPE APRICOTS
1½ CUPS SIMPLE SYRUP
½ CUP WATER
2 TABLESPOONS LEMON JUICE
1 PINCH OF SALT
¾ CUP QUALITY BRANDY

1. Split the apricots in half, remove the pits, and cut each half into thirds.
2. In three small batches, blend the apricots, simple syrup, water and lemon juice in a high-speed blender until mixture is smooth.
3. Strain through a fine-mesh sieve and discard any pulp. Whisk in salt and brandy.
4. Cover and chill thoroughly in the refrigerator. Freeze the sorbet in your ice cream machine according to the manufacturer's instructions.

## ANGEL FOOD CAKE

2 CUPS EGG WHITES, ROOM TEMPERATURE
2 CUPS SUGAR, PLUS ADDITIONAL FOR DUSTING
1 CUP FLOUR
1 TABLESPOON VANILLA
1 PINCH SALT

1. Preheat oven to 350 degrees.
2. Spray one 10-inch bundt pan or 10-12 individual mini bundt pans with cooking spray, and dust well with granulated sugar. Tap any excess sugar from the pan, and set aside.
3. Place egg whites and vanilla into bowl of a kitchenaid mixer and fit with whisk attachment. Whip on medium speed until whites are frothy, about one minute. Add half of the sugar and salt and increase to high speed, whipping until whites have reached stiff peaks.
4. Meanwhile, sift remaining sugar and flour together in small bowl.
5. Using a spatula, gently fold flour mix and meringue until batter is smooth. Place batter into bundt pan and smooth down to release air bubbles.
6. Bake until cake is golden and springs back when pressed, approximately 30-40 minutes for large pan and 16-20 minutes for individual pans.
7. Remove from oven and invert cake pan on wire rack and let cool for 30 minutes.

# BLUEBERRY CHEESECAKE ICE CREAM

## BLUEBERRY CHEESECAKE ICE CREAM

1 QUART WHOLE MILK
¾ CUP SOUR CREAM
1½ CUPS CREAM CHEESE
9 LARGE EGG YOLKS
1½ CUPS SUGAR
½ TEASPOON SALT
2 TEASPOONS VANILLA EXTRACT
½ CUP CRUSHED GRAHAM CRACKER
1 CUP BLUEBERRY PRESERVES

1. In a medium heavy-bottomed pot, combine the milk and half of the sugar. Bring the mixture to a full rolling boil.
2. Meanwhile, whisk together the remaining sugar and the egg yolks until the sugar is dissolved, about 30 seconds to one minute.
3. After the milk mixture has reached a rolling boil, carefully stream the liquid into the egg yolks, whisking constantly to prevent curdling. Add the salt, vanilla, cream cheese, and sour cream, and blend until smooth using a hand blender.
4. Chill the ice cream base on an ice bath. Refrigerate the ice cream base overnight.
5. Strain the base through a fine-mesh sieve into a clean container.
6. Freeze in an ice cream machine according to manufacturer instructions, then fold the crushed graham cracker and blueberry preserves into the ice cream before placing in the freezer.

## BLUEBERRY PRESERVES

4 CUPS BLUEBERRIES
¾ CUP PLUS 1 TABLESPOON SUGAR
1 TEASPOON LEMON JUICE
2 TABLESPOONS BALL REALFRUIT CLASSIC PECTIN

1. In medium heavy-bottomed pot, combine the blueberries, lemon juice, and ¾-cup sugar. Cook on low-medium heat stirring occasionally until the blueberries are soft and have released juice, approximately 5-10 minutes.
2. Carefully strain the mixture through a fine-mesh sieve, and set the blueberries aside to cool, and return the berry juice to the pot.
3. Meanwhile, in a separate bowl, mix together the remaining tablespoon of sugar and the pectin until combined.
4. Over medium heat, return the blueberry juice to a simmer, and whisk in the pectin mixture.
5. Cook the juice until it has come to a full boil for about one minute.
6. Pour the hot berry liquid over the cool blueberries and stir to incorporate.
7. Chill preserves over an ice bath until cool. Preserves can be used immediately, or refrigerated for several days.

## GRAHAM CRACKER

1 STICK UNSALTED BUTTER
2 TABLESPOONS DARK BROWN SUGAR
2 TABLESPOONS SUGAR
2 TABLESPOONS HONEY
1 CUP ALL PURPOSE FOUR
¼ CUP WHOLE WHEAT FLOUR
½ TEASPOON SALT
¼ TEASPOON BAKING SODA
¼ TEASPOON CINNAMON

1. In a kitchenaid mixer fitted with a paddle attachment, combine the sugars, butter, honey, and cinnamon. Cream until smooth.
2. Add the salt, baking soda, and flours. Mix until combined, scraping down the sides of the bowl once or twice to ensure the dough is homogeneous.
3. Sandwich the dough in between two pieces of parchment paper and using a rolling pin, roll the dough to about ¼-inch in thickness. Chill.
4. Once the dough is chilled, remove the top sheet of parchment paper, and bake at 350 degrees until golden brown, approximately 10 minutes, rotating halfway between baking.
5. Let graham cracker cool, then crush into pieces as desired to fold into the ice cream.

# SWEET CORN ICE CREAM with Caramel Corn Ice Cream Variation

9 LARGE EGG YOLKS
2 CUPS WHOLE MILK
2 CUPS HEAVY CREAM
¾ CUP PLUS 2 TABLESPOONS SUGAR
3 EARS YELLOW CORN ON THE COB (RAW)
¾ TEASPOON SALT
½ CUP MAPLE SYRUP

1. Remove the corn husks, if needed, and cut the corn off of the cob placing it into a small bowl. Using the back of a knife, scrape any remaining bits of kernel and corn juice from the cobs and add them to the bowl. Purée the corn and juice in a blender or food processor until smooth, and reserve in a refrigerator until needed.
2. In a medium heavy-bottomed pot, combine the milk, cream, half of the sugar, and the corn cobs. Bring the mixture to a full rolling boil.
3. Meanwhile, whisk together the sugar and the egg yolks until the sugar is dissolved, about 30 seconds to one minute.
4. After the milk mixture has reached a rolling boil, carefully stream the liquid into the egg yolks, whisking constantly to prevent curdling. Add the salt and maple syrup.
5. Chill the ice cream base on an ice bath. Once cool, add the puréed corn. Refrigerate the ice cream base overnight allowing the cobs to steep.
6. Remove the cobs from the ice cream base and strain the base through a fine-mesh sieve into a clean container.
7. Freeze in an ice cream machine according to manufacturer instructions.

*For caramel corn variation, place ¾-cup of the sugar and 2 tablespoons of water into a medium heavy-bottomed pot and cook until the sugar becomes an amber caramel. Carefully deglaze the caramel by slowly adding the milk and heavy cream while constantly whisking. Continue making the ice cream base by following the remainder of the recipe.*

# CHERRY COLA SORBET

1 POUND CHERRIES, PITTED (APPROXIMATELY 2½ CUPS)
1 PINCH OF SALT
2 TABLESPOONS LEMON JUICE
2½ CUPS COLA

1.  Combine all ingredients, and purée until smooth.
2.  Strain through a fine-mesh sieve into a clean container.
3.  Freeze in an ice cream machine according to manufacturer instructions.

# CUCUMBER-MELON GRANITA

1 LARGE HONEYDEW MELON, PEELED, DESEEDED, AND CHOPPED
2 LARGE CUCUMBERS, ROUGHLY CHOPPED
¼ CUP SIMPLE SYRUP (OR AS NEEDED)
2 TEASPOONS LEMON JUICE
1 PINCH OF SALT

1. Purée the honeydew, cucumber, lemon juice, simple syrup, and salt. Adjust sweetness based upon personal taste.
2. Strain the granita base through a fine-mesh sieve and transfer to a small baking dish.
3. Freeze the baking dish for approximately 3-4 hours, or until the mixture is completely frozen.
4. Scrape the granita with a fork to serve; it should be icy and fluffy.

# DULCE DE LECHE MILKSHAKE

2 CUPS SALTED CARAMEL ICE CREAM
1 CUP WHOLE MILK
½ TEASPOON VANILLA EXTRACT
2 TABLESPOONS CARAMEL SAUCE, PLUS EXTRA FOR GARNISH
VANILLA WHIPPED CREAM

1. In a blender (or if you are lucky enough to have a milkshake machine of your very own) combine the ice cream, milk, vanilla and caramel. For a thicker milkshake, hold back some of the milk and add as desired.
2. Blend on high until the mix is completely smooth and combined.
3. Drizzle extra caramel sauce in a cold glass. Pour in the contents of the blender.
4. Top with whipped cream. Enjoy!

## SALTED CARAMEL ICE CREAM

9 LARGE EGG YOLKS
2 CUPS WHOLE MILK
2 CUPS HEAVY CREAM
¾ CUP PLUS 2 TABLESPOONS SUGAR
¼ CUP WATER
¾ TEASPOON SALT

1. In a large heavy-bottom saucepot, combine ¾-cup sugar and water, and cook over high heat.
2. Using a heat-proof spatula, gradually stir the sugar as it begins to melt, in order to caramelize evenly. Once the sugar is fully melted, stop stirring and bring caramel to a dark amber.
3. Turn heat to low. Working carefully, pour milk and cream into the caramel. Once all of the steam subsides, turn heat back up to high, and begin to scrape any caramel that has settled on the bottom and sides of the pot.
4. Bring milk and caramel mixture to a full rolling boil, making sure all caramel is dissolved.
5. Meanwhile, whisk together the remaining 2 tablespoons of sugar and the egg yolks until the sugar is dissolved, about 30 seconds to one minute.
6. After the milk and caramel mixture has reached a rolling boil, carefully stream the liquid into the egg yolks, whisking constantly to prevent curdling. Add the salt.
7. Strain the base through a fine-mesh sieve into a clean container.
8. Chill the ice cream base on an ice bath. Refrigerate the ice cream base overnight.
9. Freeze in an ice cream machine according to manufacturer instructions.

## CARAMEL SAUCE

¾ CUP SUGAR
¾ CUP HEAVY CREAM
1 PINCH OF SALT
2 TABLESPOONS WATER
2 TABLESPOONS UNSALTED BUTTER

1. In a small heavy-bottom saucepot, combine sugar and water over medium-high heat. Cook until sugar reaches an amber color. Immediately remove from heat and carefully add heavy cream, butter and salt.
2. Strain through fine-mesh sieve into clean container. Set aside and let cool. Refrigerate up to one week, or until ready to use.

# OLIVE OIL ICE CREAM SUNDAE with Plum Preserves and Poundcake

## OLIVE OIL ICE CREAM

5 LARGE EGG YOLKS
2¼ CUPS WHOLE MILK
¾ CUP HEAVY CREAM
¾ CUP PLUS 2 TABLESPOONS SUGAR
¾ TEASPOON SALT

1. In a medium heavy-bottomed pot, combine the whole milk, heavy cream, and half the sugar. Bring the mixture to a full rolling boil.
2. Meanwhile, whisk the yolks in a large bowl. Slowly stream in the olive oil, whisking constantly until all oil is incorporated and mixture is emulsified and mayo-like in consistency. Add the remaining sugar and whisk until the sugar is dissolved, about 30 seconds to one minute.
3. After the milk mixture has reached a rolling boil, carefully stream the liquid into the egg yolk-oil mixture, whisking constantly to prevent curdling. Add the salt.
4. Strain the base through a fine-mesh sieve into a clean container.
5. Chill the ice cream base on an ice bath. Refrigerate the ice cream base overnight.
6. Freeze in an ice cream machine according to manufacturer instructions.

## PLUM PRESERVES

4 CUPS PLUMS, VARIETY OF YOUR CHOICE, SLICED (APPROXIMATELY 10-12 PLUMS)
¾ CUP PLUS 1 TABLESPOON SUGAR
1 TEASPOON LEMON JUICE
2 TABLESPOONS BALL REALFRUIT CLASSIC PECTIN

1. In medium heavy-bottomed pot combine the sliced plums, lemon juice, and ¾-cup sugar. Cook on low-medium heat stirring occasionally until the plums are soft and have released juice, approximately 5-10 minutes.
2. Carefully strain the mixture through a fine-mesh sieve, and set the plums aside to cool, and return the plum juice to the pot.
3. Meanwhile, in a separate bowl, mix together the remaining tablespoon of sugar and the pectin until combined.
4. Return the plum juice to a simmer, and whisk in the pectin mixture.
5. Cook the juice until it has come to a full boil for about one minute.
6. Pour the hot plum liquid over the cool plums and stir to incorporate.

7. Chill preserves over an ice bath until cool. Preserves can be used immediately, or refrigerated for several days.

## POUND CAKE

6 EGGS, SEPARATED
2 CUPS ALL PURPOSE FLOUR
⅛ TEASPOON BAKING SODA
1¾ CUP SUGAR, SPLIT
2 STICKS ROOM TEMPERATURE UNSALTED BUTTER
2 TABLESPOONS LEMON JUICE
1 TABLESPOON VANILLA EXTRACT
½ TEASPOON BAKING POWDER
1 PINCH OF SALT

1. In a kitchenaid mixer fitted with a paddle attachment, combine half the sugar and butter. Cream until smooth.
2. Add the egg yolks. Mix until combined, scraping down the sides of the bowl.
3. Add the salt, baking soda, baking powder, lemon juice, vanilla, and flour. Mix until combined, scraping down the sides of the bowl once or twice to ensure the dough is homogeneous. Set aside.
4. In a separate bowl, whip the egg whites until soft peaks form.
5. Slowly add the remaining sugar. Whip until medium-stiff peaks form and the meringue is glossy.
6. Carefully fold the meringue into the flour and butter mixture until incorporated and lump free.
7. Spread the pound cake batter into a parchment-lined sheet pan and bake at 350 for approximately 20-25 minutes, rotating halfway between baking until the centers springs back to the touch.
8. Let the pound cake cool, then cut into cubes of desired size to layer with scoops of olive oil ice cream and plum preserves.

# RAINBOW COOKIE ICE CREAM

2 CUPS WHOLE MILK
2 CUPS HEAVY CREAM
9 LARGE EGG YOLKS
½ CUP SUGAR
⅓ CUP HONEY
½ TEASPOON SALT

½ TEASPOON SALT
½ TEASPOONS VANILLA EXTRACT
1 TEASPOON ALMOND EXTRACT
1 CUP RAINBOW COOKIE, CHOPPED
1½ CUPS RASPBERRY JAM, SPLIT FOR THE ICE CREAM AND COOKIE

1. In a medium heavy-bottomed pot, combine the milk, cream and honey. Bring the mixture to a full rolling boil.
2. Meanwhile, whisk together the sugar and the egg yolks until the sugar is dissolved, about 30 seconds to one minute.
3. After the milk mixture has reached a rolling boil, carefully stream the liquid into the egg yolks, whisking constantly to prevent curdling. Add the salt, vanilla, and almond extract.
4. Chill the ice cream base on an ice bath. Refrigerate the ice cream base overnight.
5. Strain the base through a fine-mesh sieve into a clean container.
6. Freeze in an ice cream machine according to manufacturer instructions, then fold the rainbow cookie and raspberry jam into the ice cream to create swirls before placing in the freezer.

## RASPBERRY JAM

2½ CUPS PURÉED RASPBERRIES (APPROXIMATELY 5 CUPS WHOLE RASPBERRIES)
¾ CUP PLUS 1 TABLESPOON SUGAR
1 TEASPOON LEMON JUICE
2 TABLESPOONS BALL REALFRUIT CLASSIC PECTIN

1. In medium heavy-bottomed pot combine the raspberry purée, lemon juice, and ¾-cup sugar. Cook on low-medium heat stirring occasionally until the mix comes to a low simmer.
2. Meanwhile, in a separate bowl, mix together the remaining tablespoon of sugar and pectin until combined.
3. Slowly whisk the sugar and pectin into the raspberry mixture, whisking until it is well incorporated and lump free.
4. Increase the heat to high, bringing the mixture to a boil for about one minute.
5. Chill the jam over an ice bath until cool. Preserves can be used immediately, or refrigerated for several days.

## RAINBOW COOKIES

ONE 8-OUNCE CAN ALMOND PASTE
3 STICKS UNSALTED BUTTER
1 CUP SUGAR
4 EGGS, SEPARATED
2 TEASPOON ALMOND EXTRACT

2 CUPS ALL PURPOSE FLOUR, SIFTED
¼ CUP MILK
RED AND GREEN FOOD COLORING AS NEEDED
½ CUP RASPBERRY JAM
2 SQUARES SEMISWEET CHOCOLATE

1. In a kitchenaid mixer fitted with a paddle attachment, combine the sugar, almond paste, and one stick of butter. Mix until smooth and lump free, being sure to break down the almond paste as best you can.
2. Add the remaining butter, and continue to mix until smooth, scraping down the sides of the bowl as needed.
3. Gradually add the egg yolks, followed by the almond extract and milk. Mix until combined.
4. Add the flour and slowly mix until combined, scraping down the sides of the bowl as needed. Once the flour is combined, set aside.
5. In a separate bowl, whip the egg whites until they form stiff and fluffy peaks. Fold the whipped egg whites into the flour mixture.
6. Once the batter is smooth and combined, separate equally into three bowls.
7. Using the food coloring, dye (as desired) one bowl of batter red, another green, and leaving one bowl of batter untouched.
8. Evenly spread the batters into greased and parchment-lined quarter sheet pans and bake at 325 degrees until baked through, approximately 10 minutes, rotating each pan after 5 minutes. Let cool.
9. Once the layers are cooled, apply a thin layer of jam to the green cake and place the undyed layer directly on top, sandwiching the jam.
10. Repeat this step by applying a thin layer of jam to the undyed layer and placing the pink layer directly on top.
11. 11. Cover the cake with plastic wrap and top with one of sheet pans. Weigh down the layers with heavy plates or cans for about 4-6 hours, or overnight if possible.
12. 12. Remove the weights and plastic wrap. Melt the chocolate and spread over the top and bottom of the cake. Allow the chocolate on the top of the cake to set before flipping it over to apply the chocolate to the bottom.
13. Cut the cake into squares or rectangles as desired.

# PEACH-SHERRY GRANITA

5 LARGE RIPE PEACHES
¼ CUP SIMPLE SYRUP (OR AS NEEDED)
½ CUP SHERRY WINE (OR MORE IF DESIRED)
2 TEASPOONS LEMON JUICE
1 PINCH OF SALT

1. Purée the peaches, simple syrup, sherry, lemon juice, and salt. Adjust sweetness based upon personal taste.
2. Strain the granita base through a fine-mesh sieve and transfer to a small baking dish.
3. Freeze the baking dish for approximately 3-4 hours, or until the mixture is completely frozen.
4. Scrape the granita with a fork to serve; it should be icy and fluffy.

# BLACKBERRY-STRACCIATELLA ICE CREAM

2½ CUPS PURÉED BLACKBERRIES (APPROXIMATELY 5 CUPS WHOLE BERRIES)
5 LARGE EGG YOLKS
1 CUPS WHOLE MILK
1 CUPS HEAVY CREAM
2 TABLESPOONS HONEY
½ CUP SUGAR
¼ TEASPOON SALT
½ CUP SEMISWEET CHOCOLATE, MELTED

1. In a medium heavy-bottomed pot, combine the milk, cream, and half of the sugar. Bring the mixture to a full rolling boil.
2. Meanwhile, whisk together the remaining sugar and the egg yolks until the sugar is dissolved, about 30 seconds to one minute.
3. After the milk mixture has reached a rolling boil, carefully stream the liquid into the egg yolks, whisking constantly to prevent curdling. Add the salt.
4. Chill the ice cream base on an ice bath, and add the blackberry purée and honey. Refrigerate
5. the ice cream base overnight.
6. Strain the base through a fine-mesh sieve into a clean container.
7. Freeze in an ice cream machine according to manufacturer instructions. Before placing the ice cream into the freezer, drizzle the melted chocolate into the freshly churned ice cream, folding periodically to distribute.

# SUMMER ALE ICE CREAM with Zucchini Bread

## SUMMER ALE ICE CREAM

9 LARGE EGG YOLKS
2 CUPS SUMMER ALE
2 CUPS HEAVY CREAM
¾ CUP PLUS 2 TABLESPOONS SUGAR
¾ TEASPOON SALT

1. In a medium heavy-bottomed pot, combine the ale, cream, and half of the sugar. Bring the mixture to a full rolling boil.
2. Meanwhile, whisk together the remaining sugar and the egg yolks until the sugar is dissolved, about 30 seconds to one minute.
3. After the milk mixture has reached a rolling boil, carefully stream the liquid into the egg yolks, whisking constantly to prevent curdling. Add the salt.
4. Chill the ice cream base on an ice bath. Refrigerate the ice cream base overnight.
5. Strain the base through a fine-mesh sieve into a clean container.
6. Freeze in an ice cream machine according to manufacturer instructions.

## ZUCCHINI BREAD

2 CUPS SUGAR
3 EGGS
1  CUP VEGETABLE OIL
2 CUPS OF ALL PURPOSE FLOUR
2 TEASPOONS CINNAMON
2 TEASPOONS BAKING SODA
1½ TEASPOONS SALT
½ TEASPOON VANILLA EXTRACT
3 CUPS SHREDDED ZUCCHINI, PACKED

1. In a kitchenaid mixer fitted with a paddle attachment combine the sugar, oil, and eggs. Mix until combined.
2. Add the flour, cinnamon, salt, and baking soda.
3. Add the vanilla extract and shredded zucchini. Mix until combined, scraping down the sides of the bowl as needed.
4. Portion batter into a muffin cup-lined pan and bake at 325 degrees for 15-20 minutes, or until the cake springs bake to the touch.

# RASPBERRY-VIOLET SORBET with Lemon Cream

## RASPBERRY-VIOLET SORBET

2½ CUPS PURÉED RASPBERRIES (APPROXIMATELY 5 CUPS WHOLE BERRIES)
2 CUPS SIMPLE SYRUP
1 PINCH OF SALT
1 TABLESPOON LEMON JUICE
½ TEASPOON VIOLET EXTRACT (OR AS DESIRED)

1.  Combine all ingredients and strain through a fine-mesh sieve into a clean container.
2.  Freeze in an ice cream machine according to manufacturer instructions.

## LEMON CREAM

½ CUP SUGAR
1½ LEMONS, ZESTED
½ CUP FRESH LEMON JUICE
1 STICK BUTTER
3 LARGE EGGS
3 LARGE YOLKS
1 PINCH OF SALT
½ CUP HEAVY CREAM, WHIPPED

1.  In a medium-sized bowl, place the sugar and lemon zest. Rub the sugar and zest between your fingers to distribute the lemon oil.
2.  Place the bowl over a double boiler and add the eggs, yolks, and lemon juice.
3.  Over medium heat, cook the lemon mixture, whisking constantly until it is thick and just about able to hold a peak when the whisk is removed, approximately 5 minutes.
4.  Remove the bowl from the double boiler and add the butter, mixing until combined. Strain through a fine-mesh sieve and chill.
5.  Once the lemon curd is chilled, fold in the whipped cream until combined.
6.  Refrigerate until needed, or for 3-5 days.

# SABAYON ICE CREAM with Mixed Berry Preserves

## SABAYON ICE CREAM

9 LARGE EGG YOLKS
2 CUPS WHOLE MILK
2 CUPS HEAVY CREAM
1/3 CUP MARSALA WINE
3/4 CUP PLUS 2 TABLESPOONS SUGAR
3/4 TEASPOON SALT

1. In a medium heavy-bottomed pot, combine the milk, cream, and half of the sugar. Bring the mixture to a full rolling boil.
2. Meanwhile, whisk together the remaining sugar and the egg yolks until the sugar is dissolved, about 30 seconds to one minute.
3. After the milk mixture has reached a rolling boil, carefully stream the liquid into the egg yolks, whisking constantly to prevent curdling. Add the salt and marsala.
4. Chill the ice cream base on an ice bath. Refrigerate the ice cream base overnight.
5. Strain the base through a fine-mesh sieve into a clean container.
6. Freeze in an ice cream machine according to manufacturer instructions.

## MIXED BERRY PRESERVES

4 CUPS OF YOUR FAVORITE FRESH BERRIES
3/4 CUP PLUS 1 TABLESPOON SUGAR
1 TEASPOON LEMON JUICE
2 TABLESPOONS BALL REALFRUIT CLASSIC PECTIN

1. In medium heavy-bottomed pot combine the berries, lemon juice, and 3/4-cup sugar. Cook on low-medium heat, stirring occasionally until the berries are soft and have released juice, approximately 5-10 minutes.
2. Carefully strain the mixture through a fine-mesh sieve, and set the berries aside to cool, and return the berry juice to the pot.
3. Meanwhile, in a separate bowl, mix together the remaining tablespoon of sugar, and the pectin until combined.
4. Over medium heat, return the berry juice to a simmer, and whisk in the pectin mixture.
5. Cook the juice until it has come to a full boil for about one minute.
6. Pour the hot berry liquid over the cool berries and stir to incorporate.
7. Chill preserves over an ice bath until cool. Preserves can be used immediately, or refrigerated for several days.

# ROASTED APPLE-BACON SWIRL ICE CREAM with Pizzelle

## ROASTED APPLE-BACON SWIRL ICE CREAM

9 LARGE EGG YOLKS
2 CUPS WHOLE MILK
2 CUPS HEAVY CREAM
¾ CUP PLUS 2 TABLESPOONS SUGAR
¾ TEASPOON SALT
2 CUPS ROASTED APPLE PURÉE
¼ CUP HONEY
CANDIED BACON SWIRL, AS DESIRED

1. In a medium heavy-bottomed pot, combine the milk, cream, honey, and half of the sugar. Bring the mixture to a full rolling boil.
2. Meanwhile, whisk together the remaining sugar and the egg yolks until the sugar is dissolved, about 30 seconds to one minute.
3. After the milk mixture has reached a rolling boil, carefully stream the liquid into the egg yolks, whisking constantly to prevent curdling. Add the salt and roasted apple purée.
4. Chill the ice cream base on an ice bath. Refrigerate the ice cream base overnight.
5. Strain the base through a fine-mesh sieve into a clean container.
6. Freeze in an ice cream machine according to manufacturer instructions, then fold the bacon swirl into the ice cream before placing in the freezer.

## ROASTED APPLE PURÉE

¼ CUP SUGAR
2 TABLESPOONS DARK BROWN SUGAR
1 TEASPOON LEMON JUICE
1 LARGE PINCH OF CINNAMON
6 LARGE APPLES, SLICED INTO QUARTERS

1. Preheat oven to 350 degrees.
2. Combine sugar, brown sugar, lemon juice, and cinnamon in a medium bowl.
3. Add apples, and mix with sugar to coat.
4. Spread apples onto a parchment lined sheet pan.
5. Bake until tender but firm, 30 to 35 minutes, stirring halfway through.
6. Once the apples are cool, purée until smooth.

## CANDIED BACON SWIRL

¾ CUP BACON BITS (APPROXIMATELY 1½ CUPS GROUND BACON, UNCOOKED)
¼ CUP HEAVY CREAM
¼ CUP MAPLE SYRUP
1 CUP DARK BROWN SUGAR

1. Grind and cook bacon rendering out all of the fat, and drain.
2. In a medium heavy-bottomed pot begin to heat the maple syrup, heavy cream, and brown sugar.
3. Add the bacon to the brown sugar mixture and bring to a boil. Cook until the brown sugar is dissolved.
4. While hot, strain the mixture through a fine-mesh sieve, and chill on an ice bath.
5. Use immediately, or refrigerate for up to 1 week.

## PIZZELLE

1¾ ALL PURPOSE FLOUR
¾ CUP SUGAR
1 STICK MELTED UNSALTED BUTTER
2 TEASPOONS BAKING POWDER
1 TABLESPOON ANISE FLAVORING (OR SAMBUCA IF AVAILABLE!)
¼ TEASPOON LEMON JUICE
3 EGGS
1 PINCH OF SALT

1. In a kitchenaid mixer fitted with a paddle attachment, combine the sugar and butter. Cream until smooth.
2. Add the eggs. Mix until combined, scraping down the sides of the bowl.
3. Add the salt, flavorings, baking powder, and flour. Mix until combined, scraping down the sides of the bowl once or twice to ensure the dough is homogeneous.
4. Refrigerate until the dough is chilled.
5. Once the dough is chilled, drop about one tablespoon of batter onto each circle of a greased and heated pizzelle iron.
6. Bake for 20 to 45 seconds, or until steam is no longer coming out of the iron. Carefully remove cookies from the iron.
7. Cool completely before storing in an airtight container.

# BROWN BUTTER BRICKLE ICE CREAM

## BROWN BUTTER ICE CREAM

9 LARGE EGG YOLKS
3 CUPS MILK
1 CUP CREAM
½ CUP SUGAR
½ CUP BROWN SUGAR
¾ TEASPOON SALT
1 CUP UNSALTED BUTTER, CUT INTO SMALL PIECES
1 CUP CRUSHED BRICKLE TOFFEE

1. Place butter in a medium non-stick pot over medium-high heat.
2. Once butter is fully melted, it will foam up a bit, then subside. When the color of the butter turns a toasty brown, remove pan from heat and transfer the browned butter to a heat-proof bowl to cool.
3. When pouring the browned butter from the pot, try to leave as much of the sediment in the pot as possible. Set aside.
4. In a medium heavy-bottomed pot, combine the whole milk, heavy cream, and brown sugar. Bring the mixture to a full rolling boil.
5. Meanwhile, whisk the yolks in a large bowl. Slowly stream in the browned butter, whisking constantly, until all butter is incorporated and mixture is emulsified and mayo-like in consistency. Add the remaining sugar and whisk until the sugar is dissolved, about 30 seconds to one minute.
6. After the milk mixture has reached a rolling boil, carefully stream the liquid into the egg yolkbutter mixture, whisking constantly to prevent curdling. Add the salt.
7. Strain the base through a fine-mesh sieve into a clean container.
8. Chill the ice cream base on an ice bath. Refrigerate the ice cream base overnight.
9. Freeze in an ice cream machine according to manufacturer instructions, then fold the crushed brickle toffee into the ice cream before placing in the freezer.

## BRICKLE TOFFEE

1 CUP SUGAR
¼ CUP WATER
½ TEASPOON SALT
2 STICKS UNSALTED BUTTER

1. In a medium heavy-bottomed pot, combine all ingredients. Meanwhile, set aside a silpat or piece of parchment, and a large offset spatula on a heat-resistant surface.
2. Begin to cook the mixture over medium-high heat. Once the mixture begins to caramelize, stir constantly until a dark amber color is reached.
3. Remove the pot from the heat and carefully pour onto the prepared silpat or parchment. Immediately spread out mixture with offset spatula just until toffee is approximately ¼-inch in thickness, as overworking can cause toffee to separate.
4. Once cool, crush toffee to desired size. Store in airtight container until ready to use.

# BROWNIE SUNDAE with Sweet Milk Sorbet and Miso Milk Jam

## BROWNIE

3 STICKS UNSALTED BUTTER
1 CUP DARK CHOCOLATE
6 EGGS
3 CUPS SUGAR
1½ TEASPOONS VANILLA
2 CUPS FLOUR
1½ TEASPOONS SALT

1. Melt butter and chocolate in a medium bowl over a double boiler. Whisk until smooth and silky, and set aside.
2. In a small bowl, whisk half of the sugar with flour and salt.
3. In a large bowl, whisk remaining sugar with eggs and vanilla.
4. Pour melted chocolate into the sugar and egg mixture, and whisk until smooth.
5. Fold in flour until brownie batter is homogenous.
6. Pour batter into a greased 9 x 13 pan and bake at 325 degrees for 25 to 30 minutes, until the top of the brownies have set and crack slightly on the edges, or a toothpick inserted into the brownies has only moist crumbs on it.
7. Let cool, or if you're the gooey brownie sundae type, serve warm with scoops of sweet milk sorbet and a generous drizzle of miso milk jam.

## SWEET MILK SORBET

3 14-OZ. CANS SWEETENED CONDENSED MILK
3½ CUPS NONFAT SKIM MILK

1. Combine all ingredients in a clean container, whisking until smooth.
2. Freeze in an ice cream machine according to manufacturer instructions.

## MISO MILK JAM

4 CUPS MILK
2 CUPS SUGAR
¼ CUP HONEY
1 VANILLA BEAN, SPLIT AND SCRAPED
½ CUP RED MISO

1. In a large saucepan over medium-high heat, combine the milk, sugar, honey and vanilla bean and bring to a boil, stirring occasionally to prevent burning, about 5 minutes.
2. Reduce the heat to medium low and cook, stirring frequently to prevent scorching, until the mixture has reduced and turned amber in color, about 25 minutes.
3. Once the mixture has reached the desired caramel color, remove from heat and stir in the red miso.
4. Let cool and keep refrigerated in an airtight container up to one week.

# BURNT HONEY ICE CREAM with Fennel-Hazelnut Shortbread

## BURNT HONEY ICE CREAM

9 LARGE EGG YOLKS
2 CUPS WHOLE MILK
2 CUPS HEAVY CREAM
1¼ CUP HONEY
¾ TEASPOON SALT

1. In a medium heavy-bottomed pot, place 1 cup of the honey.
2. Over medium heat, cook the honey until it turns a dark amber color, 3-5 minutes.
3. Carefully deglaze the honey by whisking in the heavy cream and milk. Bring the mixture to a full rolling boil.
4. Meanwhile, whisk together the remaining honey and the egg yolks until the honey is dissolved, about 30 seconds to one minute.
5. After the milk mixture has reached a rolling boil, carefully stream the liquid into the egg yolks, whisking constantly to prevent curdling. Add the salt.
6. Chill the ice cream base on an ice bath. Refrigerate the ice cream base overnight.
7. Strain the base through a fine-mesh sieve into a clean container.
8. Freeze in an ice cream machine according to manufacturer instructions.

## FENNEL-HAZELNUT SHORTBREAD

¾ CUP ALL PURPOSE FLOUR
1 CUP HAZELNUT FLOUR, OR HAZELNUT MEAL
¼ TEASPOON SALT
½ CUP CONFECTIONER'S SUGAR
1 TABLESPOON DARK BROWN SUGAR
½ TEASPOON VANILLA EXTRACT
½ TEASPOON GROUND FENNEL SEED
1½ STICKS UNSALTED BUTTER
SUGAR IN THE RAW AS NEEDED

1. In a kitchenaid mixer fitted with a paddle attachment, combine the sugars and butter, and cream until smooth.
2. Add the remaining ingredients and mix just until combined.
3. Sandwich the dough in between two pieces of parchment paper, and using a rolling pin, roll the dough to about ¼-inch in thickness. Chill.
4. Once the dough is chilled, punch into rounds or cut into desired shape and place on a greased and lined sheet pan. Sprinkle with sugar in the raw.
5. Bake at 350 degrees until golden brown, approximately 8 minutes, rotating halfway between baking.
6. Serve with generous scoops of burnt honey ice cream.

# CINNAMON ROLL ICE CREAM

## CINNAMON ROLL ICE CREAM

9 LARGE EGG YOLKS
2 CUPS WHOLE MILK
2 CUPS HEAVY CREAM
15-20 CINNAMON STICKS

¾ CUP PLUS 2 TABLESPOONS SUGAR
¾ TEASPOON SALT
1 CUP CINNAMON ROLL CUBES
½ CUP CREAM CHEESE SWIRL

1. In a medium heavy-bottomed pot, combine the milk, cream, cinnamon sticks, and half of the sugar. Bring the mixture to a full rolling boil.
2. Meanwhile, whisk together the remaining sugar and the egg yolks until the sugar is dissolved, about 30 seconds to one minute.
3. After the milk mixture has reached a rolling boil, carefully stream the liquid into the egg yolks, whisking constantly to prevent curdling. Add the salt.
4. Chill the ice cream base on an ice bath. Refrigerate the ice cream base overnight allowing the cinnamon sticks to steep.
5. Strain the base through a fine-mesh sieve into a clean container.
6. Chill the ice cream base on an ice bath. Refrigerate the ice cream base overnight.
7. Freeze in an ice cream machine according to manufacturer instructions, then fold the cinnamon roll cubes, followed by cream cheese swirl, into the ice cream before placing in the freezer.

## CINNAMON ROLL

¾ STICK UNSALTED BUTTER
1 LARGE EGG
1 TEASPOON VANILLA EXTRACT
1½ TEASPOON SALT
¼ CUP SUGAR
3 ¾ CUP ALL-PURPOSE FLOUR

1½ CUPS MILK, ROOM TEMPERATURE
3¼ TEASPOONS ACTIVE DRY YEAST, OR 4½ TABLESPOONS FRESH YEAST, IF AVAILABLE
½ STICK SOFT UNSALTED BUTTER, FOR ASSEMBLING CINNAMON ROLL

1. In a kitchenaid mixer fitted with paddle attachment, combine yeast and milk. Mix until combined.
2. Add flour, sugar, salt, egg and vanilla, and mix on medium speed for 5-8 minutes until dough is smooth and begins to pull away from sides of the bowl.
3. Form the dough into a smooth ball and place in a greased stainless steel bowl. Cover the bowl with plastic wrap and let the dough rest in a warm place until it has doubled in size, approximately 30 minutes.
4. Once the dough has doubled in size, turn it out onto a floured work surface, and lightly flour top of dough.
5. Using a rolling pin, gently roll dough into a rectangular shape, approximately 15 x 9 inches.
6. Spread soft butter over dough, and cover liberally with cinnamon sugar mixture.
7. Starting at the 15-inch side, roll up dough and pinch edges together to seal. Cut into 12 pieces.
8. Grease the bottom of a 9 x 13 inch baking pan. Evenly place cinnamon roll slices in pan. Cover with plastic wrap and let rise until dough has doubled in size, approximately 45 minutes to 1 hour.
9. Bake in 350 degree oven for 15-20 minutes, until golden brown.
10. Remove from oven and let cool.

## CINNAMON ROLL SUGAR

1 CUP BROWN SUGAR
1 CUP SUGAR
¼ CUP CINNAMON
½ TEASPOON SALT

1. Combine all ingredients together. Store in an airtight container until ready to use.

## CREAM CHEESE SWIRL

8 OUNCES CREAM CHEESE
¼ CUP SUGAR
1 TEASPOON VANILLA
¼ TEASPOON SALT
2 TEASPOONS HEAVY CREAM

1. In a kitchenaid mixer fitted with a paddle attachment, combine cream cheese and sugar. Mix on high speed until sugar is dissolved and batter is fluffy.
2. Add the remaining ingredients. Mix until combined scraping down the sides of the bowl.

# SPICED PEAR SORBET with Black Pepper Scone

## SPICED PEAR SORBET

8 MEDIUM PEARS, ABOUT 2 POUNDS
1 750-mL BOTTLE RED WINE
3 CUPS WATER
3¾ CUPS SUGAR
¼ CUP CARDAMOM PODS
2 TABLESPOONS WHOLE BLACK PEPPER
10 CINNAMON STICKS
10 WHOLE CLOVES
5 WHOLE STAR ANISE

1. Peel and core pears, and set aside.
2. Create a sachet with the cardamom, pepper, cinnamon stick, clove and star anise. Trim a piece of cheesecloth large enough to hold the spices, then cut a piece of twine or string long enough to tie the sachet together. Lay out the cheesecloth and place the spices on it, then fold the cheesecloth and tie the packet together, making sure there are no gaps where the spices can fall out.
3. Combine red wine, water, sugar and spice sachet in large pot over high heat, and bring mixture to a boil, stirring to combine the sugar.
4. Gently add pears to red wine poach, and reduce heat to medium-low. Simmer until pears are tender when pierced with a fork, 10-15 minutes.
5. Remove pot from heat and let pears cool completely in poaching liquid.
6. Transfer entire mixture into a container, cover and let sit overnight.
7. In small batches, blend pears in a high-speed blender until smooth. Strain the purée through a fine-mesh sieve into a clean container.
8. Whisk in 2 cups of spiced poaching liquid with pear purée. Freeze the mixture in your ice
9. cream machine according to the manufacturer's instructions.

## BLACK PEPPER SCONE

3½ CUPS BREAD FLOUR, PLUS EXTRA FOR DUSTING
½ CUP BROWN SUGAR, PACKED
2 TABLESPOONS BAKING POWDER
2 TEASPOONS FRESHLY GROUND BLACK PEPPER
½ TEASPOON SALT
1 CUP PLUS 2 TABLESPOONS CREAM, PLUS EXTRA FOR BAKING
SUGAR IN THE RAW, FOR BAKING

1. In a large bowl, whisk together flour, sugar, baking powder, pepper, and salt.
2. Make a well in the center of your flour mixture, and pour the cream into it.
3. Stir gently with a fork or spatula until scone dough just comes together, being very careful not to overmix.
4. Turn the scone dough out onto a lightly floured surface. Pat the dough into a circle about 1-inch thick.
5. Cut the scones with a sharp knife or pastry dough cutter, and place onto a parchment-lined baking sheet.
6. Brush scones with cream and sprinkle with sugar in the raw, and if you love a little heat, crack some extra black pepper on top!
7. Bake scones in a 400 degree oven for 15-20 minutes until light golden brown.
8. Let cool slightly and serve warm with spiced pear sorbet

# MAPLE-WALNUT ICE CREAM

9 LARGE EGG YOLKS
2 CUPS WHOLE MILK
2 CUPS HEAVY CREAM
2 CUPS PURE MAPLE SYRUP
1 TABLESPOON SUGAR
¾ TEASPOON SALT
1 CUP WALNUTS, TOASTED AND ROUGHLY CHOPPED

1. In a large pot over medium-low heat, cook down the maple syrup at a low simmer until it has reduced by half.
2. Once the maple has reduced, add the milk and cream. Bring the mixture to a full rolling boil.
3. Meanwhile, whisk together the sugar and the egg yolks until the sugar is dissolved, about 30 seconds to one minute.
4. After the milk mixture has reached a rolling boil, carefully stream the liquid into the egg yolks, whisking constantly to prevent curdling. Add the salt.
5. Chill the ice cream base on an ice bath. Refrigerate the ice cream base overnight.
6. Strain the base through a fine-mesh sieve into a clean container.
7. Freeze in an ice cream machine according to manufacturer instructions, then fold the toasted walnuts into the ice cream before placing in the freezer.

# PUMPKIN SPICE LATTE MILKSHAKE

2 CUPS PUMPKIN SPICE ICE CREAM
1 CUP WHOLE MILK
1 SHOT ESPRESSO, OR 1 OUNCE STRONG BREWED COFFEE, COOLED
VANILLA WHIPPED CREAM
GINGERSNAPS
GROUND CINNAMON FOR GARNISH

1. In a blender (or if you are lucky enough to have a milkshake machine of your very own) combine the ice cream, milk, and espresso. For a thicker milkshake, reserve some of the milk and add as desired.
2. Blend on high until the mix is completely smooth and combined.
3. Pour the contents into a cold glass.
4. Top with whipped cream and gingersnaps. Enjoy!

## PUMPKIN SPICE ICE CREAM

9 LARGE EGG YOLKS
2 CUPS WHOLE MILK
2 CUPS HEAVY CREAM
2 CUPS PUMPKIN PURÉE
2 CUPS MAPLE SYRUP
2 TABLESPOONS SUGAR

1½ TEASPOONS GROUND NUTMEG
1½ TEASPOONS GROUND CINNAMON
¾ TEASPOON GROUND GINGER
¾ TEASPOON GROUND CLOVE
¾ TEASPOON SALT

1. In a medium heavy-bottomed pot, combine the milk, cream, spices, and maple syrup. Bring the mixture to a full rolling boil.
2. Meanwhile, whisk together the sugar and the egg yolks until the sugar is dissolved, about 30 seconds to one minute.
3. After the milk mixture has reached a rolling boil, carefully stream the liquid into the egg yolks, whisking constantly to prevent curdling. Add the salt and pumpkin purée, and blend until smooth using a hand blender.
4. Chill the ice cream base on an ice bath. Refrigerate the ice cream base overnight.
5. Freeze in an ice cream machine according to manufacturer instructions.

## VANILLA WHIPPED CREAM

1 CUP HEAVY CREAM
1 TEASPOON VANILLA EXTRACT
2 TEASPOONS CONFECTIONER'S SUGAR

1. In a kitchenaid mixer fitted with a whip attachment, combine the cream, vanilla, and sugar.
2. Beat at medium speed until medium-stiff peaks form.
3. Use immediately, or refrigerate for several hours until needed.

## GINGERSNAPS

1½ STICKS UNSALTED BUTTER
1 CUP SUGAR
1 EGG
1 TABLESPOON GRATED FRESH GINGER ROOT
¼ CUP MOLASSES

2 CUPS ALL PURPOSE FLOUR
1 TEASPOON CINNAMON
½ TEASPOON SALT
1½ TEASPOONS BAKING SODA
CANDIED GINGER AND SUGAR IN THE RAW FOR GARNISHING

1. In a kitchenaid mixer fitted with a paddle attachment, combine the sugars and butter, and cream until smooth.
2. Add the egg, ginger, and molasses. Mix until combined, scraping down the sides of the bowl.
3. Add the remaining ingredients and mix just until combined.
4. Sandwich the dough in between two pieces of parchment paper and using a rolling pin, roll the dough to about ¼-inch in thickness. Chill.
5. Once the dough is chilled, punch into rounds or desired shape and place on a greased and lined sheet pan. Sprinkle with sugar in the raw and candied ginger.
6. Bake at 350 degrees until golden brown, approximately 8 minutes, rotating halfway between
7. baking.
8. 7. Let cookies cool before garnishing milkshake.

# SUGAR COOKIE ICE CREAM

## SPICED PEAR SORBET

9 LARGE EGG YOLKS
3 CUPS WHOLE MILK
1 CUP HEAVY CREAM
¾ CUP PLUS 2 TABLESPOONS SUGAR
2 TEASPOONS VANILLA EXTRACT
¾ TEASPOON SALT
3½ CUPS SUGAR COOKIE CRUMBS
¼ CUP RAINBOW SPRINKLES

1. In a medium heavy-bottomed pot, combine the whole milk, heavy cream, and half of the sugar. Bring the mixture to a full rolling boil.
2. Meanwhile, whisk together the remaining sugar and the egg yolks until the sugar is dissolved, about 30 seconds to one minute.
3. After the milk mixture has reached a rolling boil, carefully stream the liquid into the egg yolks, whisking constantly to prevent curdling. Add the salt, vanilla, and three cups sugar cookie crumbs and blend until smooth using a hand blender.
4. Chill the ice cream base on an ice bath. Refrigerate the ice cream base overnight.
5. Strain the base through a fine-mesh sieve into a clean container.
6. Freeze in an ice cream machine according to manufacturer instructions, then fold the remaining half-cup of sugar cookie crumbs and rainbow sprinkles into the ice cream before placing in the freezer.

## SUGAR COOKIE

3⅓ CUP ALL PURPOSE FLOUR
¾ TEASPOON SALT
1¼ CUPS CONFECTIONER'S SUGAR
1 TABLESPOON VANILLA EXTRACT
3 STICKS UNSALTED BUTTER

1. In a kitchenaid mixer fitted with a paddle attachment, combine the sugar and butter, cream until smooth.
2. Add the remaining ingredients and mix just until combined.
3. Sandwich the dough in between two pieces of parchment paper and using a rolling pin, roll the dough to about ¼-inch in thickness. Chill.
4. Once the dough is chilled, remove the top sheet of parchment and bake at 350 degrees until golden brown and baked through, approximately 10-15 minutes, rotating halfway between baking.
5. Let cool before crushing into crumbs.

# PECAN PIE ICE CREAM

9 LARGE EGG YOLKS
2 CUPS WHOLE MILK
2 CUPS HEAVY CREAM
¾ CUP PLUS 2 TABLESPOONS DARK BROWN SUGAR
¾ TEASPOON SALT
1 CUP TOASTED PECANS
¼ MAPLE SYRUP
½ CUP CANDIED PECANS, ROUGHLY CHOPPED
½ CUP BROWN SUGAR SYRUP
½ CUP BROKEN UP PIECES PIE CRUST

1. Blend toasted pecans and milk in high-speed blender.
2. In a large heavy-bottom saucepot, combine the toasted pecan milk, cream, half of the brown sugar, and maple syrup. Bring the mixture to a full rolling boil.
3. Meanwhile, whisk together the remaining brown sugar and egg yolks until the sugar is dissolved, about 30 seconds to one minute.
4. After the milk mixture has reached a rolling boil, carefully stream the liquid into the egg yolks, whisking constantly to prevent curdling. Add the salt.
5. Strain the base through a fine-mesh sieve into a clean container. Cool the ice cream base on an ice bath.
6. Freeze in an ice cream machine according to manufacturer instructions, then fold the candied pecans, pie crust, and brown sugar syrup into the ice cream before placing in the freezer.

## BROWN SUGAR SYRUP

¼ CUP HEAVY CREAM
¼ CUP MAPLE SYRUP
1 CUP DARK BROWN SUGAR
1 PINCH OF SALT

1. In a medium heavy-bottomed pot, combine all ingredients, and begin to heat.
2. Bring the brown sugar mixture to a boil and cook until the brown sugar is dissolved.
3. While hot, strain the mixture through a fine-mesh sieve, and chill on an ice bath.
4. Use immediately, or refrigerate for up to 1 week.

## CANDIED PECANS

1 CUP PECAN HALVES
3 TABLESPOONS WATER
3 TABLESPOONS SUGAR
1 PINCH OF SALT

1. Preheat oven to 300 degrees.
2. Mix sugar, water, and salt together in a bowl.
3. Toss pecans in the sugar mixture
4. Bake pecans on a parchment-lined sheet pan, stirring every 5-10 minutes until pecans are evenly browned, about 20-30 minutes.

## PIE CRUST

1½ CUPS ALL PURPOSE FLOUR
2 STICKS UNSALTED BUTTER, COLD AND CUBED
½ CUP ICE WATER
1 PINCH OF SALT
1 PINCH OF GRATED NUTMEG
1 TEASPOON SUGAR

1. Combine the flour, salt, nutmeg, and sugar in a large bowl and stir briefly until the mixture is combined.
2. Using a pastry blender or your fingers, cut the butter into the dry ingredients until it is in peasize pieces.
3. Drizzle in the ice water gradually and mix just until the dough comes together, using only as much water as needed.
4. Let the dough relax for a minimum for 1-2 hours, or longer if possible.
5. Sandwich the pie dough in between two pieces of parchment paper and using a rolling pin, roll the dough to about ¼-inch in thickness. Chill.
6. Once chilled, remove the top sheet of parchment paper and bake pie dough at 350 degrees until golden brown, about 20-30 minutes.
7. Let cool, then break into piece before using, or store in an airtight container.

# DIRTY CHAI ICE CREAM

9 LARGE EGG YOLKS
2 CUPS WHOLE MILK
2 CUPS HEAVY CREAM
¾ CUP PLUS 2 TABLESPOONS SUGAR
1 TEASPOON VANILLA EXTRACT
¼ TEASPOON WHOLE PEPPERCORNS, SLIGHTLY CRUSHED
¼ TEASPOON WHOLE CLOVES, SLIGHTLY CRUSHED
1½ TEASPOONS WHOLE CARDAMOM PODS, SLIGHTLY CRUSHED
1½ TABLESPOONS FRESH GINGER
1 CUP BREWED ESPRESSO
¾ TEASPOON SALT
3 CINNAMON STICKS

1. In a medium heavy-bottomed pot, combine the milk, cream, half of the sugar, cloves, peppercorns, cardamom pods, ginger, and cinnamon sticks. Bring the mixture to a full rolling boil.
2. Meanwhile, whisk together the remaining sugar and the egg yolks until the sugar is dissolved, about 30 seconds to one minute.
3. After the milk mixture has reached a rolling boil, carefully stream the liquid into the egg yolks, whisking constantly to prevent curdling. Add the salt.
4. Chill the ice cream base on an ice bath. Refrigerate the ice cream base overnight allowing the spices to steep.
5. Strain the base through a fine-mesh sieve into a clean container and add the brewed espresso.
6. Freeze in an ice cream machine according to manufacturer instructions.

# VANILLA-RUM ICE CREAM ROOT BEER FLOAT

## VANILLA-RUM ICE CREAM

9 LARGE EGG YOLKS
2 CUPS WHOLE MILK
2 CUPS HEAVY CREAM
3 VANILLA BEANS, SPLIT AND SCRAPED
¾ CUP PLUS 2 TABLESPOONS SUGAR
¾ TEASPOON SALT
3 OUNCES DARK RUM

1. In a small bowl, rub together the vanilla bean pods, vanilla bean pith and sugar until they are combined well and the sugar is speckled with vanilla.
2. In a medium heavy-bottomed pot, combine the milk, cream and half of the sugar. Bring the mixture to a full rolling boil.
3. Meanwhile, whisk together the remaining sugar and the egg yolks until the sugar is dissolved, about 30 seconds to one minute.
4. After the milk mixture has reached a rolling boil, carefully stream the liquid into the egg yolks, whisking constantly to prevent curdling. Add the salt.
5. Chill the ice cream base on an ice bath. Refrigerate the ice cream base overnight allowing the vanilla pods to steep.
6. Strain the base through a fine-mesh sieve into a clean container.
7. Freeze in an ice cream machine according to manufacturer instructions.
8. Scoop ice cream into the glass of your choice. Top with the root beer and enjoy!

# HORCHATA ICE CREAM with Rumchata Variation

9 LARGE EGG YOLKS
2 CUPS WHOLE MILK
2 CUPS HEAVY CREAM
¾ CUP PLUS 2 TABLESPOONS SUGAR
¾ CUP LONG GRAIN RICE
¼ TEASPOON CINNAMON
¾ TEASPOON SALT

1. Put rice in heavy-bottom non-stick skillet, and place over medium-high heat.
2. Using a wooden spoon, stir rice gradually as it starts to heat, and more frequently once the pan is very hot and rice begins to gain color. Toast rice until golden brown and smells fragrant and nutty.
3. Remove pan from heat, and immediately pour toasted rice into a bowl to cool.
4. Blend toasted rice and milk in high-speed blender, and strain through a fine-mesh sieve.
5. In a large heavy-bottom saucepot, combine the toasted rice milk, cream, half of the sugar, and cinnamon. Bring the mixture to a full rolling boil.
6. Meanwhile, whisk together the remaining sugar and egg yolks until the sugar is dissolved, about 30 seconds to one minute.
7. After the milk mixture has reached a rolling boil, carefully stream the liquid into the egg yolks, whisking constantly to prevent curdling. Add the salt.
8. Strain the base through a fine-mesh sieve into a clean container. Cool the ice cream base on an ice bath.
9. Freeze in an ice cream machine according to manufacturer instructions.

*For rumchata variation, toast an extra ¼-cup of rice, increase cinnamon to ¾ teaspoon, and add half of one vanilla bean pod, split and scraped. Once ice cream base is cool, add 3 cups of dark rum, or more if you'd like it boozy-licious! Continue making the ice cream base by following the remainder of the recipe.*

# EGGNOG ICE CREAM with Gingerbread

## EGGNOG ICE CREAM

9 LARGE EGG YOLKS
2 CUPS WHOLE MILK
2 CUPS HEAVY CREAM
2½ TEASPOONS FRESHLY GRATED NUTMEG
¾ CUP PLUS 2 TABLESPOONS SUGAR
¾ TEASPOON SALT
1½ OUNCES DARK RUM
1½ OUNCES WHISKEY

1. In a medium heavy-bottomed pot, combine the milk, cream, nutmeg, and half of the sugar. Bring the mixture to a full rolling boil.
2. Meanwhile, whisk together the remaining sugar and the egg yolks until the sugar is dissolved, about 30 seconds to one minute.
3. After the milk mixture has reached a rolling boil, carefully stream the liquid into the egg yolks, whisking constantly to prevent curdling. Add the salt, rum and whiskey.
4. Chill the ice cream base on an ice bath. Refrigerate the ice cream base overnight.
5. Strain the base through a fine-mesh sieve into a clean container.
6. Freeze in an ice cream machine according to manufacturer instructions.

## GINGERBREAD

2 CUPS PLUS 2 TABLESPOONS ALL PURPOSE FLOUR
1½ TEASPOONS BAKING SODA
1 TEASPOON GROUND CINNAMON
1 TABLESPOON PLUS 1 TEASPOON GROUND GINGER
½ TEASPOON SALT
3 LARGE EGGS
¾ CUP MOLASSES
½ CUP DARK BROWN SUGAR
¼ CUP SUGAR
¾ CUP GRAPESEED OR VEGETABLE OIL
½ CUP WATER

1. In a kitchenaid mixer fitted with a paddle attachment, combine the sugars and eggs on medium-low speed, beating until homogenous.
2. Add the molasses, oil, and water. Mix until combined.
3. Add the remaining ingredients to the bowl. Mix until combined, scraping down the sides of the bowl as needed to ensure the batter is smooth.
4. Bake the batter in desired vessel at 350 degrees until the cake springs back to the touch, approximately 20 minutes for muffins, and 15 minutes for a half sheet pan. Serve warm!

# BANANA-MALT ICE CREAM WHOOPIE PIES

Sandwich generous scoops of banana-malt ice cream between whoopie pies and enjoy!

## BANANA-MALT ICE CREAM

9 LARGE EGG YOLKS
2 CUPS WHOLE MILK
2 CUPS HEAVY CREAM
¾ CUP PLUS 2 TABLESPOONS SUGAR
¾ TEASPOON SALT
¼ CUP MALTED MILK POWDER
½ CUP BARLEY MALT SYRUP
1 CUP BANANA, PURÉED

1. In a medium heavy-bottomed pot, combine the whole milk, heavy cream, malted milk powder, and half of the sugar. Bring the mixture to a full rolling boil.
2. Meanwhile, whisk together the remaining sugar and the egg yolks until the sugar is dissolved, about 30 seconds to one minute.
3. After the milk mixture has reached a rolling boil, carefully stream the liquid into the egg yolks, whisking constantly to prevent curdling. Add the salt, barley malt syrup, and banana purée.
4. Chill the ice cream base on an ice bath. Refrigerate the ice cream base overnight.
5. Strain the base through a fine-mesh sieve into a clean container.
6. Freeze in an ice cream machine according to manufacturer instructions.

## WHOOPIE PIES

1 CUP SUGAR
½ STICK UNSALTED BUTTER
1 EGG
½ CUP BUTTERMILK
½ CUP PLUS 2 TABLESPOONS WARM WATER
½ TEASPOON VANILLA EXTRACT
2 CUPS ALL PURPOSE FLOUR
¼ CUP PLUS 2 TABLESPOONS COCOA POWDER
1 TEASPOON BAKING SODA
½ TEASPOON SALT

1. In a kitchenaid mixer fitted with a paddle attachment, combine the sugar and butter, and cream until the mixture is light and fluffy.
2. Add the egg and vanilla extract. Mix until combined, scraping down the sides of the bowl.
3. Add the remaining ingredients, alternating the wet and dry. Be sure to scrape down the sides of the bowl during additions to ensure the batter is smooth.
4. Using a piping bag fitted with a number 4 plain tip, pipe the whoopie batter onto silpats into rounds approximately 1-2 inches in diameter, or as desired
5. Bake at 300 degrees until the whoopies spring back to the touch and are uniform in color, approximately 8-10 minutes, rotating halfway between baking.
6. Let cool.

# ROASTED PINEAPPLE SORBET with Carrot Cake

## ROASTED PINEAPPLE SORBET

1 LARGE PINEAPPLE, PEELED, CORED, AND CHOPPED
½ CUP SUGAR
3 TABLESPOONS WATER
2 CUPS DRY WHITE WINE
1 PINCH OF SALT
½ VANILLA BEAN, SCRAPED

1. Mix sugar, water, and vanilla bean with pod in a deep medium saucepan, and bring to a boil over medium-high heat until the sugar starts to caramelize.
2. Gently swirl the pan to even out the caramel and prevent burning.
3. Continue to cook until the sugar turns medium amber in color.
4. Carefully place the pineapple into the caramel and deglaze with the white wine.
5. Place the pan with the pineapple into a 350 degree oven and roast for approximately 8-10 minutes until the pineapple is tender.
6. Let the pineapple cool completely and discard the vanilla bean pod.
7. Blend the pineapple and roasting liquid in a high speed blender until smooth, then strain the base through a fine-mesh sieve into a clean container.
8. Freeze in an ice cream machine according to manufacturer instructions.

## CARROT CAKE

2 CUPS SUGAR
3 EGGS
1⅓ CUP VEGETABLE OIL
2 CUPS ALL PURPOSE FLOUR
2 TEASPOONS CINNAMON
2 TEASPOONS BAKING SODA
1½ TEASPOONS SALT
½ TEASPOON VANILLA EXTRACT
3 CUPS SHREDDED CARROTS, PACKED

1. In a kitchenaid mixer fitted with a paddle attachment combine the sugar, oil, and eggs. Mix until combined.
2. Add the flour, cinnamon, salt, and baking soda.
3. Add the vanilla extract and shredded carrot. Mix until combined, scraping down the sides of the bowl as needed.
4. Portion batter into a muffin cup-lined pan and bake at 325 degrees for 15-20 minutes, or until the cake springs bake to the touch.

# COCONUT CURRY-CASHEW CRUNCH ICE CREAM

9 LARGE EGG YOLKS
2 CUPS COCONUT MILK
2 CUPS HEAVY CREAM
¾ CUP PLUS 2 TABLESPOONS SUGAR
¾ TEASPOON SALT
2 CUPS DESICCATED COCONUT
1 TEASPOON MADRAS CURRY POWDER
¾ CUP CHOPPED CASHEW BRITTLE

1. In a medium heavy-bottomed pot, combine the coconut milk, heavy cream, desiccated coconut, curry, and half of the sugar. Bring the mixture to a full rolling boil.
2. Meanwhile, whisk together the remaining sugar and the egg yolks until the sugar is dissolved, about 30 seconds to one minute.
3. After the milk mixture has reached a rolling boil, carefully stream the liquid into the egg yolks, whisking constantly to prevent curdling. Add the salt.
4. Chill the ice cream base on an ice bath. Refrigerate the ice cream base overnight.
5. Strain the base through a fine-mesh sieve into a clean container.
6. Freeze in an ice cream machine according to manufacturer instructions, then fold the crushed cashew brittle into the ice cream before placing in the freezer.

## CASHEW BRITTLE

1 CUP SUGAR
2 TABLESPOONS WATER
2 TABLESPOONS LIGHT CORN SYRUP
½ STICK UNSALTED BUTTER
2 TEASPOONS SALT
¼ TEASPOON BAKING SODA
½ CUP CASHEWS, COARSELY CHOPPED AND TOASTED

1. In a medium heavy-bottomed pot, combine the sugar, water, corn syrup, and butter. Meanwhile, set aside two silpats or pieces of parchment, and a rolling pin on a heat-resistant surface.
2. Begin to cook the mixture over medium heat, watching carefully until it becomes a light amber color. Be sure to not stir or agitate the mixture once it begins to boil to avoid crystallizing.
3. Once the caramel has reached the desired color, lower the heat and add the baking soda and salt (the mix will foam up slightly). Mix until combined and continue to cook until the caramel is a medium amber color, about 30 second to one minute.
4. Remove the pot from the heat and carefully stir in the cashews. Pour immediately onto the prepared silpat or parchment, topping with the second silpat or piece of parchment paper.
5. Using the rolling pin, roll out the sandwiched brittle until it is about ¼-inch in thickness and uniform. Let cool, and break into pieces, as you desire. Store in an airtight container for 1-2 weeks.

# PASSIONFRUIT MARGARITA SORBET

1 CUP PASSION FRUIT PUREE
¼ CUP PLUS 1 TABLESPOON TEQUILA
2½ CUPS SIMPLE SYRUP
HALF OF A SMALL ORANGE, JUICED
1 LIME, JUICED
1 PINCH OF SALT
1¼ CUPS WATER

1.  Combine all ingredients and strain through a fine-mesh sieve into a clean container.
2.  Freeze in an ice cream machine according to manufacturer instructions.

# CREAMSICLE ICE CREAM

9 LARGE EGG YOLKS
2 CUPS WHOLE MILK
2 CUPS HEAVY CREAM
¾ CUP PLUS 2 TABLESPOONS SUGAR
¼ CUP ORANGE JUICE
ZEST OF ONE ORANGE
2 VANILLA BEANS, SPLIT AND SCRAPED
¾ TEASPOON SALT

1.  In a small bowl, rub together the orange zest, vanilla bean pods, vanilla bean pith and sugar until they are combined well and the sugar is speckled with vanilla.
2.  In a medium heavy-bottomed pot, combine the milk, cream, and half of the sugar. Bring the mixture to a full rolling boil.
3.  Meanwhile, whisk together the remaining sugar and the egg yolks until the sugar is dissolved, about 30 seconds to one minute.
4.  After the milk mixture has reached a rolling boil, carefully stream the liquid into the egg yolks, whisking constantly to prevent curdling. Add the salt.
5.  Chill the ice cream base on an ice bath. Once cool, add the orange juice. Refrigerate the ice cream base overnight allowing the vanilla pods and orange zest to steep.
6.  Strain the base through a fine-mesh sieve into a clean container.
7.  Freeze in an ice cream machine according to manufacturer instructions.

# GIANDUJA ICE CREAM with Espresso Waffle

## GIANDUJA ICE CREAM

9 LARGE EGG YOLKS
2 CUPS WHOLE MILK
2 CUPS HEAVY CREAM
¾ CUP PLUS 2 TABLESPOONS SUGAR
¾ TEASPOON SALT
½ CUP CHOPPED DARK CHOCOLATE
½ CUP CHOPPED MILK CHOCOLATE
¼ CUP HAZELNUT PASTE
½ CUP CHOPPED TOASTED HAZELNUTS

1. Place the milk and dark chocolate in a large bowl and set aside.
2. In a medium heavy-bottomed pot, combine the milk, cream, and half of the sugar. Bring the mixture to a full rolling boil.
3. Meanwhile, whisk together the remaining sugar and the egg yolks until the sugar is dissolved, about 30 seconds to one minute.
4. After the milk mixture has reached a rolling boil, carefully pour half of the hot milk over chocolate, and whisk until chocolate is completely combined.
5. Add the remaining hot milk and whisk together. Add salt and hazelnut paste.
6. Strain the base through a fine-mesh sieve into a clean container.
7. Chill the ice cream base on an ice bath. Refrigerate the ice cream base overnight.
8. Freeze in an ice cream machine according to manufacturer instructions, and fold in chopped hazelnuts before placing in the freezer.

## ESPRESSO WAFFLE

4½ CUPS ALL PURPOSE FLOUR
½ TEASPOON BAKING SODA
2 TEASPOONS SALT
1 TABLESPOON GROUND ESPRESSO
2 TABLESPOONS DRY YEAST
3 CUPS WARM MILK
4 EGGS
¼ CUP BREWED ESPRESSO
1½ STICKS MELTED UNSALTED BUTTER

1. In a kitchenaid mixer fitted with paddle attachment, mix flour, baking soda, salt, espresso, dry yeast, and warm milk until smooth and combined. Cover with plastic wrap and let rest until mixture has doubled in size.
2. Once mixture has doubled, whip eggs in a separate bowl until light and ribbon-like, approximately three minutes.
3. Gently fold eggs into flour mixture, followed by brewed espresso and butter.
4. Cook waffle batter according to waffle iron manufacturer instructions.
5. Scoop generous amount of ice cream onto warm waffle. Enjoy!

# CHOCOLATE SODA FLOAT

2 SCOOPS MILK CHOCOLATE ICE CREAM

¼ CUP COCOA SYRUP, OR MORE IF YOU'RE A CHOCOHOLIC!

CLUB SODA, OR CARBONATED BEVERAGE OF CHOICE

1. Fill a tall chilled glass with milk chocolate ice cream scoops.
2. Pour the cocoa syrup over the ice cream.
3. Fill the glass by slowly pouring the soda over the ice cream and syrup.
4. Top generously with whipped cream and chocolate shavings and enjoy with a long spoon and straw.

## MILK CHOCOLATE ICE CREAM

9 LARGE EGG YOLKS

2 CUPS WHOLE MILK

2 CUPS HEAVY CREAM

¾ CUP PLUS 2 TABLESPOONS SUGAR

¾ TEASPOON SALT

½ CUP CHOPPED DARK CHOCOLATE

½ CUP CHOPPED MILK CHOCOLATE

1. Place the milk and dark chocolate in a large bowl and set aside.
2. In a medium heavy-bottomed pot, combine the milk, cream, and half of the sugar. Bring the mixture to a full rolling boil.
3. Meanwhile, whisk together the remaining sugar and the egg yolks until the sugar is dissolved, about 30 seconds to one minute.
4. After the milk mixture has reached a rolling boil, carefully pour half of the hot milk over chocolate, and whisk until chocolate is completely combined.
5. Add the remaining hot milk and whisk together. Add salt.
6. Strain the base through a fine-mesh sieve into a clean container.
7. Chill the ice cream base on an ice bath. Refrigerate the ice cream base overnight.
8. Freeze in an ice cream machine according to manufacturer instructions.

## COCOA SYRUP

1 CUP WATER

½ CUP PLUS 2 TABLESPOONS COCOA POWDER

¾ CUP SUGAR

¼ CUP HEAVY CREAM

1. Place all of the ingredients into a heavy-bottomed pot and mix to combine.
2. Bring the mixture to a boil over medium-low heat.
3. Strain the cocoa syrup through a fine-mesh sieve into a clean container.
4. Chill on an ice bath.
5. Use immediately, or refrigerate for up to 1 week.

# LIME SHERBET

2 CUPS LIME JUICE
2 CUPS GREEK YOGURT
1 PINCH OF SALT
¼ CUP HONEY
2½ CUPS SIMPLE SYRUP

1.  Combine all ingredients and strain through a fine-mesh sieve into a clean container.
2.  Freeze in an ice cream machine according to manufacturer instructions.

## SIMPLE SYRUP

2 CUPS SUGAR
2 CUPS WATER

1.  In a heavy bottomed pot combine the sugar and water.
2.  Bring to a rolling boil to ensure the sugar is dissolved. Chill and refrigerate.

# RED VELVET MILKSHAKE

2 CUPS RED VELVET ICE CREAM
1 CUP WHOLE MILK
1 TEASPOON COCOA POWDER
VANILLA WHIPPED CREAM
RED VELVET CAKE CRUMBS

1. In a blender (or if you are lucky enough to have a milkshake machine of your very own) place the ice cream, milk, and cocoa powder. For a thicker milkshake, reserve some of the milk and add as desired.
2. Blend on high until the mix is completely smooth and combined.
3. Pour the contents into a cold glass.
4. Top with whipped cream and red velvet cake crumbs. Enjoy!

## RED VELVET ICE CREAM

9 LARGE EGG YOLKS
3 CUPS WHOLE MILK
1 CUP HEAVY CREAM
¾ CUP PLUS 2 TABLESPOONS SUGAR
¾ TEASPOON SALT
2½ TO 3 CUPS (225 GRAMS) RED VELVET CAKE

1. In a medium heavy-bottomed pot, combine the milk, cream, and half of the sugar. Bring the mixture to a full rolling boil.
2. Meanwhile, whisk together the remaining sugar and the egg yolks until the sugar is dissolved, about 30 seconds to one minute.
3. After the milk mixture has reached a rolling boil, carefully stream the liquid into the egg yolks, whisking constantly to prevent curdling. Add the salt and red velvet cake. Blend until smooth using a hand blender.
4. Chill the ice cream base on an ice bath. Refrigerate the ice cream base overnight.
5. Strain the base through a fine-mesh sieve into a clean container.
6. Freeze in an ice cream machine according to manufacturer instructions.

## RED VELVET CAKE

3½ CUPS ALL PURPOSE FLOUR
1½ STICKS UNSALTED BUTTER
2¼ CUPS SUGAR
3 LARGE EGGS
⅓ CUP COCOA POWDER
1½ TEASPOONS SALT
1½ TEASPOONS WHITE VINEGAR
1½ TEASPOONS BAKING SODA
1½ TEASPOONS VANILLA EXTRACT
2 CUPS BUTTERMILK
RED FOOD COLORING AS DESIRED

1. Preheat your oven to 350 degrees.
2. In a kitchenaid mixer fitted with a paddle attachment, cream the butter and sugar together until they are light in color and fluffy.
3. Add the eggs one at a time, mixing and scraping down the sides of the bowl with each addition.
4. Add the cocoa powder, vanilla, food coloring, salt, vinegar, and baking soda. Mix until combined.
5. Add the flour, alternating with the buttermilk.
6. Mix until combined, scraping well throughout.
7. Bake in a greased and parchment lined half sheet pan until the center springs back to the touch, approximately 20 minutes, rotating halfway between baking.

## RED VELVET CAKE

1 CUP HEAVY CREAM
1 TEASPOON VANILLA EXTRACT
2 TEASPOONS CONFECTIONER'S SUGAR

1. In a kitchenaid mixer fitted with a whip attachment, combine the cream, vanilla, and sugar.
2. Beat at medium speed until medium-stiff peaks form.
3. Use immediately, or refrigerate for several hours until needed.

# SPICED COOKIE ICE CREAM

18 LARGE EGG YOLKS
6 CUPS WHOLE MILK
2 CUPS HEAVY CREAM
1¾ CUP SUGAR
1½ TEASPOON SALT
2½ TO 3 CUPS SPICED COOKIE, CRUSHED

1. In a medium heavy-bottomed pot, combine the whole milk, heavy cream, and half of the sugar. Bring the mixture to a full rolling boil.
2. Meanwhile, whisk together the remaining sugar and the egg yolks until the sugar is dissolved, about 30 seconds to one minute.
3. After the milk mixture has reached a rolling boil, carefully stream the liquid into the egg yolks, whisking constantly to prevent curdling. Add the salt and spiced cookie, and blend until smooth using a hand blender.
4. Chill the ice cream base on an ice bath. Refrigerate the ice cream base overnight.
5. Strain the base through a fine-mesh sieve into a clean container.
6. Freeze in an ice cream machine according to manufacturer instructions.

## SPICED COOKIE

1 STICK UNSALTED BUTTER
¾ CUP SUGAR
1¼ CUPS ALL PURPOSE FLOUR
2 TABLESPOONS MOLASSES
1 EGG
1½ TEASPOONS GROUND CINNAMON
¾ TEASPOON GROUND NUTMEG
¾ TEASPOON GROUND CARDAMOM
¾ TEASPOON GROUND CLOVE
⅛ TEASPOON GROUND GINGER
1 TEASPOON BAKING POWDER
1 TEASPOON SALT

1. In a kitchenaid mixer fitted with a paddle attachment, combine the sugar and butter, and cream until smooth.
2. Add the egg and molasses. Mix until combined, scraping down the sides of the bowl.
3. Add the remaining ingredients and mix until combined.
4. Sandwich the dough in between two pieces of parchment paper and using a rolling pin, roll the dough to about ¼-inch in thickness. Chill.
5. Once the dough is chilled, remove the top sheet of parchment and bake at 350 degrees until golden brown and baked through, approximately 10-15 minutes, rotating halfway between baking.
6. Let cookie cool.

# ROSEMARY-GRAPEFRUIT SORBET

1 CUP GRAPEFRUIT JUICE
1½ CUPS SIMPLE SYRUP
½ CUP WATER
2 LARGE FRESH ROSEMARY SPRIGS
1 TEASPOON LIME JUICE
1 PINCH OF SALT

1. In a medium heavy bottomed pot bring the simple syrup to a boil and add the rosemary sprigs. Turn off the heat and steep for 15-20 minutes. Strain.
2. Combine the remaining ingredients.
3. Freeze in an ice cream machine according to manufacturer instructions.

# BAKED ALASKA with Cherry-Vanilla Ice Cream and Devil's Food Cake

## BAKED ALASKA

1. Spray a 5-cup capacity baking bowl with cooking spray and line with plastic wrap, allowing a little to hang over the edge.
2. Using a cookie cutter, or by hand, cut out a circle of devil's food to fit the bottom of the bowl, and press cake firmly in.
3. Top with freshly-spun ice cream, smoothing with a spatula to make sure there are no air bubbles.
4. Cut out a circle of devil's food to fit on top of the ice cream. This should fit just at the top of the bowl, and no ice cream should leak out.
5. Cover assembled cake with plastic wrap overhang, using extra if needed to cover any exposed cake, and freeze for at least 4 hours, and up to 24 hours.
6. To remove the assembled cake from bowl, open plastic wrap, flip bowl upside down and gently release cake onto a baking sheet, and remove plastic wrap. Return the cake to the freezer while making the meringue.
7. making the meringue.

## CHERRY-VANILLA ICE CREAM

9 LARGE EGG YOLKS
2 CUPS WHOLE MILK
2 CUPS HEAVY CREAM
3 VANILLA BEANS, SPLIT AND SCRAPED

¾ CUP PLUS 2 TABLESPOONS SUGAR
¾ TEASPOON SALT
1 CUP OF YOUR FAVORITE CHERRY JAM, OR POACHED CHERRIES LISTED BELOW

1. In a small bowl, rub together the vanilla bean pods, vanilla bean pith and sugar until they are combined well, and the sugar is speckled with vanilla.
2. In a medium heavy-bottomed pot, combine the milk, cream, and half of the sugar. Bring the mixture to a full rolling boil.
3. Meanwhile, whisk together the remaining sugar and the egg yolks until the sugar is dissolved, about 30 seconds to one minute.
4. After the milk mixture has reached a rolling boil, carefully stream the liquid into the egg yolks, whisking constantly to prevent curdling. Add the salt.
5. Chill the ice cream base on an ice bath. Refrigerate the ice cream base overnight allowing the vanilla pods to steep.
6. Strain the base through a fine-mesh sieve into a clean container.
7. Freeze in an ice cream machine according to manufacturer instructions, then fold the cherry jam into the ice cream before placing in the freezer.

## POACHED CHERRIES

½ CUP SUGAR
½ CUP RED VERJUS OR RED WINE

1 PINCH OF SALT
1 CUP DRIED OR PITTED FRESH CHERRIES

1. Combine all ingredients in a medium heavy-bottom pot. Bring mixture to a boil and let simmer 3-5 minutes.
2. Remove from heat and let cool.
3. Once cool, place poached cherries in a food processor or blender. Blend until cherries are broken down and chunky, or smoother if desired. Refrigerate up to 1 week or until ready to use.

## DEVIL'S FOOD CAKE

7 CUPS SUGAR
4 CUPS FLOUR
1½ TEASPOONS BAKING SODA
1¼ TEASPOONS BAKING POWDER
3 STICKS UNSALTED BUTTER, MELTED

6 EGGS
1 TEASPOON VANILLA
1 CUP PLUS 3 TABLESPOONS COCOA POWDER
1½ CUPS PLUS 2 TABLESPOONS WARM WATER

1. Preheat oven to 350 degrees.
2. In a small bowl, whisk together flour, baking powder, and baking soda. Set aside.
3. In bowl of an electric mixer fitted with the whisk attachment, combine sugar and melted butter. Whisk on medium speed until combined.
4. Add eggs and vanilla and whisk to combine.
5. Add cocoa powder and mix in.
6. Add water and flour mixture to batter, alternating and scraping down the sides of the bowl after each addition until smooth.
7. Evenly spread the batter into a greased and parchment-lined half sheet pan and bake until cake is set, about 15-20 minutes, rotating pan after 10 minutes. Remove from oven, and let cool on a wire rack.

## SWISS MERINGUE

4 LARGE EGG WHITES
1 CUP SUGAR

1. Heat egg whites and sugar in a kitchenaid bowl over a double boiler, whisking consistently, until sugar dissolves and mixture is very hot to the touch, about 2 minutes.
2. Transfer bowl to kitchenaid mixer, and whisk until stiff and glossy peaks form, about 5 minutes.
3. Remove cake from freezer and cover with desired amount of meringue.
4. Hold a small handheld kitchen torch 2 to 3 inches from surface of meringue. Torch meringue until dark golden and toasted. Alternatively, carefully place cake in 500-degree oven and bake until meringue is browned, 2 to 3 minutes.
5. Slice and serve immediately, or return to freezer until ready. Enjoy!

*Alternatively, meringue can be made using a heatproof bowl and an electric hand mixer.*